Goddess Spirituality Book
Rituals, Holydays and Moon Magic

Diana Voigt
Literarische Agentur
A-1010 Wien, Hoher Markt 1
T +43/1/533 31 91 F +43/1/533 31 92
e-mail: voigtlit @ ping.at

Previously published as
"Wild Witches Don't Get The Blues"

By Ffiona Morgan

✪
Daughters of the Moon Publishing
P.O. Box 81, Graton, Ca. 95444   (707) 829-5248

Daughters of the Moon Publishing
Box 81, Graton, Ca. 95444
(707) 829-5248.

CONTRIBUTORS

Cover Design and Painting byFfiona Morgan.
Art from Daughters of the Moon Tarot
(Send for free brochure to address above)
Other Art Contributors: Jean Van Slyke, Rainbow, Max Daschu,
and Judith Hower (Turtle Hill Studios, POB 1064,
Forestville, Ca. 95436, (707) 887-1414)
Norma Joyce for her extensive contribution and love,
To Martha Courtout who offered her most wonderful writing
Baba Copper for Lunar Resonance Meditation
Ila Suzanne for her poetry throughout the book
Moontree for her story, Shekhinah for her poem,
Janet Seaforth, my Tai Chi teacher, for her story

Editing by Susan Mermaid, Ellen Rifkin, Judith Hower,
Margaret Wheat, Snake, Artemis, LeAnne and Robin Watson

Thanks to:

Heartfelt thanks to all wimmin who worked on this
book, especially Robi McGowan and the editors
Love to Artemis, my partner, for all her work and ongoing support
Yolanda and Claudia for their input on racist language.
Rosamond, My Crone, I love you
I thank Lorna for emotional support and love; also
Glenda, Merit, Noreen, and my children,

Copyright © 1991, 1992, 1995
By Ffiona Morgan

About the Author

Ffiona Morgan is a wild Welsh witchwomon who loves the Goddess and the earth with a passion. This is the third of her self-publishing efforts, her first being the enormously successful Daughters of the Moon Tarot (book and deck), and the second being "Wild Witches Don't Get The Blues". After twenty years of ritual and womon's spirituality as both a seeker and a Priestess, she publishes this sacred book during her fifty-third year of life.

The author has an M.A. in Women's Studies and Social Science, and extensive experience as an astrologer, ritualist, crystal expert, and tarot reader. She has also created "Magical Crystals", which correlate with color healing, astrological energies, and tarot.

The name "Ffiona" symbolizes "light of the moon", "Morgan" is Goddess of the darkness, visions, automatic writing and things that are not possible, "fading out" of lost cultures, languages and boundaries between the worlds. Morgan will pick you as her own, as she picked Ffiona.

Ffiona grew up with her Welsh immigrant grandparents in a tiny town in Saskatchewan, Canada and came to the U.S. when she was twenty years old. Besides reading and writing books, she loves baby goats, radical feminism, dancing, singing, wild country, and wild wimmin.

The author is available for workshops and rituals on the wide variety of topics you will find in this book. Contact: Daughters Of The Moon, P.O. Box 81, Graton, CA. 95444. (707) 829-5248. Information on how to obtain Magical Crystals and Daughters of the Moon Tarot available from the same source.

CONTENTS

Homeself, Sacredself

I would counsel you to be still
To move away from everything for a time
To wait quietly until you come home to yourself

There will be signs
Songs will sing from your lips
Your body will dance with you
Your eyes will see magic
Where you keep the fresh flower
Where you burn the candle
Also where you cry and where you bleed

There will be signs
The magic of your homeself, your sacredself
Will take you to the sky
Luna will welcome your flight with silver embraces
Comets will be your lovers
Trails of stars will carry you inward
Until, at your core, a cataclysm will burst
In celebration of homecoming
To the magic of your soul

Ila Suzanne

I wrote this book exclusively in "the female" as a step in reclaiming ourselves. We, as wimmin, have been omitted, erased and made invisible in the language, history and culture of our peoples. Since there are no words that describe both sexes (except "people"), wo**men** have been included in the male gender—**man**kind, hu**man**, etc. "He" is meant to mean "man and wo**man**." All of the root words for wo**men** contain the word man; **she** contains "he", fe**male** contains "male". Throughout this book I have spelled wo**man** and wo**men** various other ways—womon, womoon,.wombon, wemoon, wimmin, womyn. This is not by accident, but to make a point. It is to address the inequality and imbalance that exists, and to correct it.

INTRODUCTION

The Goddess is at last being rediscovered. She is rising from the memories of wimmin after being closeted for over 2,000 years. She has been waiting to ascend and take Her rightful place as the soul of our living earth. Patriarchy only wants to remember Her as The Virgin Mary, (a obvious takeover of Isis worship), but we who are her lovers, remember her as the Mother of all life. Her worship is found in the European Pagan religion, called The Craft Of The Wise, or Wicce, which is an earth religion with its home in nature. European Pagans saw all life forms as sacred, and therefore did not honor their Goddesses through violence or sacrifice. **The Craft,** (the name I will use for Wicce throughout this book) virtually disappeared after the Inquisition when the Christian Catholic Church murdured millions of witches.

This book is written from the perspective of "Dianic Wicce", which means practising The Craft exclusively with wimmin. There also exists a very large Pagan network, which includes groups for womyn and men.

When invoking The Goddess for healing or other assistance, please remember that She will do her share, but we must also do ours, simultaneously working in concert to create a desired reality. For example: If I pray to the Goddess for love and I am sincere, She will help me receive love. However, I must also open myself, take the initiative and show others I love them, and any other action that will facilitate love entering my life. I don't just sit back and wait for it to happen.

The biggest lie of the patriarchy is that the Earth is not alive. We know that The Goddess lives, that Her body **is** the earth. She also lives inside each one of us. We are connected to Her tides with our bleeding and she is the beauty within us, our very best. Our living, breathing physical body is a reflection of the living, breathing body of the earth.: we are a microcosm of the macrocosm, which is our planet. This is beautifully expressed in the Wicce concept of "Goddess Within, Goddess Without" which is a recognition that She exists as the world, and also exists inside each one of us, a living embodiment. As we realize that what we have been taught is so horrendously untrue, another veil is lifted and our whole perspective changes: there is no turning back.

Chant
She changes everything She touches
And everything She touches, changes.
Changes . . .. Touches. . .. Touches. . ..Changes. . .
(repeat and repeat)

Starhawk

We can then behold our beautiful world with eyes that really see the trees breathing, the water singing, the rocks speaking, and the air vibrating with Her graceful dance. We know The Goddess lives, manifesting Her Sacredself in the rich earth, in the skies and waters, and inside each one of us. She is the beauty and goodness we see in every womon – the best we have to offer.

This is a womanspirit book in honor of the Earth. It is to share what I have intiutively been given and taught about rituals, crystals, the elements, and life, by womyn and The Divine. It is written with the hope that we can all change and learn to care for Mother Earth, all Her creatures and each other.

I gift you with Redwing's song, a song that I have sung for many years:

The Earth, She Is My Mother

The Earth, She is My Mother.
Her rivers the blood that nourishes me.
Her trees, help me to breathe
And her plants heal my body and soul.

The Earth has many deep wounds
Her rivers are dammed, Her breath has been poisoned
Her body has been raped, Many children left
homeless......
And Still.......Her Magic is everywhere!!

The Earth She has taught me to heal myself,
And soon, she will heal Her own wounds,
Many, many mountains will move.....
The Earth will shake, the dams will break....
The poisons will disappear....
The Earth my Mother shall be no one's land
The Earth shall be no one's land.
                    by Redwing, Albion,1976

This is a book of Earth Magic—of "working" (to cast a spell while doing a ritual is to "work" magic), with the natural elements of The Goddess. It is about the magic that surrounds us; in the air we breathe, the water we drink, the clay from which we shape our pots. It is my gift—where I can share what I have intuitively been given and also taught by others, about rituals, crystals, the elements, life, and The Goddess. My hope is that all peoples of this earth will grow strong and loving, learning to live gently on Mother Earth and care for all Her creatures.

I wish this offering to be a prayer, a gift of love to all of you who have come into my life, and touched me with your beauty.

To those of you, my sisters, who have hurt me, I forgive you.

To those of you, my sisters, who I have hurt, please forgive me.

Long before scientists and advocates of the widely–known Gaia theory, (which "proves" to linear, scientific minds that our earth is a living organism), pagans and witches were celebrating her joy, wonder and beauty. The concept of our Earth as a living, breathing, female body, with every human, animal and plant being individual cells in Her body, is revolutionary in itself, because once you have recognized the earth as your extended body, it is much more difficult to participate in the pollution, carelessness, and exploitation that has become a way of life in contemporary culture. We are not only killing the earth with this laziness and lack of concern, but we are killing ourselves. It all comes home, to you, and to that plastic bag that you have to wash and recycle each day. This is your earth, what will you do **to** Her? **For** Her? You can't change others but you can change the way you live gently on this planet or add to Her murder.

Hawaii is the land of a quite recent matriarchal civilization, the presence of The Goddess there is very evident. When you visit The Big Island, among the erupting volcanos and strong earth energy, you can feel the power and vitality of Pele, fire-breathing volcano Goddess (see graphic, p. 21). On that fiery mountain of Kilueau you can readily feel Her sacred energy and have easy access to Her holy body, the body on which you walk every day. Realize that you do so *only* by her infinite grace and compassion . . . that any time She so chooses, She could wipe out the entire human race with a puff of Her magnificent breath or a raging volcanic fire from Her fingertips.

All the crimes of mankind are inflicted on Her body, which is covered with concrete. Her sacred breath, the air, is polluted with exhaust fumes and toxic gases. Garbage and untreated waste are spewed into her healing waters, the oceans and rivers. When I am in pain or depressed, I know I am also feeling the pain of The Mother, and I know She is suffering as I am. But in the midst of her suffering I see that still her magic, that exists in such splendor, is everywhere!!

As a species we have regressed to our present level of consciousness. We are only beginning to fully comprehend the damage that has been done, and to remember what the Earth once looked like. There are some things which we can do to halt this destruction, One of them is to recycle, organize to stop the slaughter of the rainforests, which provide much of our oxygen, and ask Her for forgiveness. We become humble at the immensity of Her power and beauty. Send Her love in ritual circles and as a daily ritual; just as She sends us love every moment by allowing us, by the grace of Her being, to exist on this earth, Her body.

My first introduction to magic was through my study of the psychic. (Back then, 20 years ago, we called magic "psychic work".) That meant using my mind to visualize and create realities. Some of the material I have gathered is unpublished; I have credited my sources of knowledge whenever I knew them, and some has been passed along, both in Wiccan circles and women's medicine circles. If you see something that came from you and is unacknowledged, please write me and I will give you credit in the next printing. Blessed Be—also expressed as "Aloha Aina, Mitakuye Oyasin, Mame-Ioshn and Ho!"

Ffiona Morgan, California, November, 9994.

Being Goddess

Being Goddess is being able to
recognize within one's Self
The things that are important,
And then to strike the single note
That brings them into alignment
WIth everything else that exists.

Then beyond moral or logic or esthetics,
One is wind or fire, the sea, the mountains, rain, the Moon,
The Sun or the stars, the flight of an arrow,
The end of a day, the embrace of a lover.
Those who look upon you then say,

Without even knowing your names,
'She is Fire, She is Dance, She is Destruction, She is Love'
You may not call yourself Goddess,
Everyone else does though,
Everyone who beholds you.

Author unknown

The Return of the Goddess
by Starhawk

The Goddess...once was awake in us...But a time came...when in some places the people turned away from Her. Men ruled... They waged endless wars. Many of the people, especially the women, resisted...The Goddess was fettered, beaten, raped, tortured, burned, poisoned and dismembered.

And so the earth herself nearly died. But though the Goddess suffered, she was never destroyed... her memory was...never forgotten. In secret, some continued to practice the old ways.

And in the time when the final destruction of earth seemed probable...those seeds began to sprout.... to remember the Goddess, the Witches arose and danced in the open. But the ending of this myth is not yet written. Has the Goddess reawakened only to preside over the destruction of the earth? Or will our awakening come in time?

"This is our answer: our language is poetry. Do you understand? Our language is signs, symbols, sacred objects; we are a sacred people. We have magical properties.

We tell you this: we are doing the impossible. We are teaching ourselves to be human. When we are finished, the strands which connect us will be unbreakable; already we are stronger than we have ever been. The fibers which we weave on our insides will be so tight nothing will be able to pass through them.

We tell you this: when we are finished, we will be a proud people. We are making ready, as we send ourselves out separately across the dying continent. Holding on to shells, stones, feathers, amulets, we are taking on their properties.

Thus we move: silently, separately; our name is buried in various sacred spots all over the land. We are waiting until it is safe to claim it. Though we move silently, separate, can you hear our joint voices singing, singing our women's songs in ever widening circles?

Listen. We are making ready. Hear our music across the dying land..."

From _Tribe_ by Martha Courtout

Chapter 1
The Magical Path

CHAPTER 1
THE MAGICAL PATH OF THE GODDESS

Blessed be, blessed be
Circle, circle, ring of time
Sing the song, say the rhyme
Round and round, three times three
Secret space–So mote it be
Ila Suzanne

INTRODUCTION TO RITUAL

Ritual is when time and space, as we know it, are dissolved and we enter sacred time. We are at one and equal with every womon who enters this time with us. "Sometimes we are self-conscious about creating or participating in ritual. We are of two minds: the spirit deeply longs for communion with the sacred; the public self is maintained by withholding emotional intensity".[1] We gather the materials and sacred tools that will evoke the feelings, images, and memories of the deep mind needed for ritual.

"Magic is how everything comes to be....magic is knowing you make a difference...Magic is working with mind, heart, and psychic energy....fire, water, air, earth and aether. Magic can be done together or alone....in a temple, at home, or in the wilderness....any place that feels special and sacred. Magic is myth and visions of fantasy, casting spells, understanding herbs and the mysterious forces of planets, moon and stars. It can be done in pure innocence or great knowing. "If it harms none, do as thou wilt" is the cardinal rule of magic...use it for good and you will become good, use it for ill and you will become ill. Magic is the oldest wisdom, it is folk-knowledge—it belongs to everybody."[2]

Wicce, or Goddess worship, declares that all acts of love and pleasure are Her rituals. When you transform your everyday work into a ritual, it empowers you. This means that when you bake bread with love you are performing a ritual, when you bathe or light altar candles you perform acts of self-love, which are all acts of love and pleasure. It means that sex is not sinful or dirty but an act of love in worship of The Mother. It means that your work (hopefully an act of pleasure) is a ritual.

"We have a concept of *Ache. Ache* means power, not power to dominate anyone, but the power to run your body, to think, to create, just the power to be. Ritual is primarily done for the purpose of pulling *ache* from the universe, having guidance on how to use *ache*, and then to give that *ache* back to the universe. jTo circulate, renew, use, attract, and commune with power is the primary reason for all rituals. Ritual is stylized in order that it becomeS a habit."[3]

Through ritual we satisfy our need to be connected with the Goddess and each other. It is also a way to create community and experience ourselves in a deep way. To be able to do magic is to feel in tune with the Earth through our unconscious connection with Her. We have those memories deep within, from the past, and through ritual we bring them to the surface.

What are we trying to accomplish with ritual? One answer is to commune with the Goddess, to become more like Her, and recognize Her energy in us. Through ritual we reclaim our heiitage and power.

Women are starved for spirituality; that is a fact. The mainstream culture, now so "hip" about racism and reclycling, crystals and UFO's, does not carry its New Age Understanding to paganism and witchcraft. One of the most disgusting images presented by patriarchy is that of the ugly, old witch with the wart on her nose. It is hatred of not only witches but of all womyn, and especially hatred of the old wimmin, the Crones, third aspect of the Goddess.

RITUALS
By Norma Joyce

"Ritual celebrations are for women wanting to join together in a circle. All of them include raising the cone of power. A ritual is a physical expression of an emotion or belief that a group of women come together to share, and is repeated time after time within the group.

"What is a circle? Energy? Blessing?

"Have you sat quietly and listened to yourself? I don't mean the words of the ongoing inner-talking dialogue or chatter. Move past the words and listen to the movement that makes a sound—it is the movement of energy within us. When we are more fully acquainted with this movement we can hear it humming. That energy can be gathered and used for many positive purposes, from healing to getting a job. Remember the old saying, 'Watch what you ask for, you might get it.' I find it best to be very clear about my needs and wants, remembering to add, 'Only if this is in the best interest of myself and the universe.' The energy is an inward force, but it is also outer in that we are constantly receiving energy from all living entities and giving it off. The more we learn to direct that energy and join it with other women, the more we are able to be in charge of our fate.

"The blessing or rainbow light is energy in yet another form. With this form of visualizing, rather than hearing, we visualize the cosmic force, creative energy, or Goddess power. We visualize the rainbow light protecting, enfolding, and giving love to ourselves and others. We also feel its energy; it is a creation of our being that takes form.

"The circle is the form in which we develop these senses and learn to use them. Learning how to move energy in a group, around the circle, until it becomes a spiral of upward motion, a cone of power, is a wonderful tool for deep understanding and for magical workings. The workings can be healings or additional energy for someone who is going through a difficult time.

"Giving energy does not make you feel depleted if you learn to cleanse and filter the energy that comes back to you from others. Energy that is not cleansed can make you feel drained. Sometimes, when I am interacting with another, I will feel drained, and I will then realize they are energy-takers who cannot give back, and that I have forgotten to flood myself with energy. At such times, if I remember to center, I can receive positive energy from an animal or a plant in the room. The rainbow energy is important for cleansing and protecting.

Don't be afraid to start a circle because you don't think many women will be interested. When a pupil is ready to learn the teacher will arrive. So it is when you start a circle, and when you start visualizing energy, others will feel the positive vibrations coming from you and respond. A circle can be done with the utmost simplicity, starting with clasping of each other's hands, visualizing, and feeling the energy. The next step is to learn to move the energy and use it for positive purposes. A circle can include rituals that are meaningful to everyone; the group can use candles and incense, or other helpers that facilitate receptivity.

"I think it is very important for us women to be able to love ourselves, or at least be in the process of learning, for we cannot love others until we learn to love ourselves.

"Since the energy is high and cleansed after a circle, it is a good time to do other things; for example, a past-life regression or tarot/astrology readings. "Soft" eyes are a way of looking/non-looking. When driving a car, reading, doing those kind of things, we are using "hard eyes". Soft eyes are almost unfocused, not quite, but almost. They allow our visual object to change; thus, we see it in a different perspective. When your eyes are open in a ritual, you will want to use soft eyes as much as possible."

DIANIC WICCAN ETHICS

Ethics is a frequently discussed issue among feminist witches. I do not know any feminists who do "negative" spells, to hurt others. There is a reason for this—none of us who believe in the threefold law of witchcraft (that whatever you do comes back to you three times) want to have negative magic come back on us! I know there are groups of satanists out there doing negative magic and many times these are the groups the media points out when they speak of "witchcraft". I hereby deny any association with any of these groups; as feminist witches we abhor all forms of violence. We hold sacred the earth and all her wonder. This includes spells to manipulate others: if you manipulate with spells, you will be manipulated, and three times over. I don't wish for such a fate; neither do my sisters. If you do a spell for someone, ask permission beforehand. Always add to any spell, "Only if you wish it, and it be for the best."

Another important principle of Wicce is the concept of "What is true above is also true below", meaning that the principles that are alive in my inner life are also alive in the world. My attitudes, how I think and view things are a measure of how others will treat me and how I will feel about life.

I AM

I am the Maker, I am the Shaper
She is the Power, let it go.
I am the Dreamer, I am the Dancer,
She is the Movement, let it flow.
She is the Power, She is the Movement,
Let it flow through you, Pass it on.
Sister to Sister, mother to daughter
Let it flow through you and pass it on.

I am the Channel, I am the River,
She is the Ocean, hear Her roar.
I am the Seed and I am the Flower,
She is the Spring Rain, see Her pour.
She is the Ocean, She is the Spring Rain,
Let it flow through you, Pass it on.
Sister to sister, mother to daughter,
Let it flow through you and pass it on.

I am the Garden, I am the Forest,
She is the Bright Sun, see it gleam
I am the Night Sky, I am the Good Earth,
She is the Full Moon, see it beam.
She is the Bright Sun, She is the Full Moon,
Let it flow through you, Pass it on.
Sister to sister, mother to daughter,
Let it flow through you and pass it on.

Power to Movement, Ocean to Storm Cloud,
Let it flow through you, pass it on.
Bright Sun to Full Moon, cycle to cycle,
Let it flow through you and pass it on.

Susan Humphreys

THE PENTACLE

In Wicce, The Pentacle is seen as a positive symbol. It is first seen as a circle of life with the human body in the center of the circle. The five points of the pentacle represent the head (upper point), the two arms (side points) and two feet (bottom points). The circle surrounding the Pentacle represents the earth, which surrounds the human being.

The Pentacle has been misused and usurped as a symbol of negative magic by groups calling themselves "Satanists". Thus, the association of The Pentacle with negative magic, or evil, has been planted in the minds of many people of this country. We, as positive practitioners, still wish to claim the image and power of the pentacle as a symbol of goodness and a life-producing craft.

The Pentacle also represents the Five Elements. In the diagram below the Center, or Aether, element is the upper point, representing Spirit. The two horizontal points are correlated with Water (feelings, emotions), the West, for the left arm, and Air (mind, intellect) The East, for the right arm of the Pentacle. The two bottom points, or legs, of the Pentacle represent North, which is Earth (body, material plane) as its left leg, and South, or Fire (action, will) as the right leg.

Center
Spirit

West
Water

East
Intellect

North
Earth

South
Fire

**THE SACRED PENTACLE
OF LIFE**

MAIDEN, MOTHER AND CRONE ARCHETYPES

An important concept that goes back to earlier days of Goddess worship is the concept of Maiden, Mother, Crone, or the idea of The Triple Goddess.

Many cultures embody these three faces or aspects in one Goddess, just as we womyn have them within us. Some of these goddesses are: The Three Fates, The Norns, The Gorgons, The Erzulie, The Graces, The Furies, Zoryas, Maries, The Morrigan, Bhavani and Triple Pussa. There are also many Goddesses whose functions or aspects are exclusively that of a Maiden, Mother or Crone. Because of Her many names and functions, She is called "The Goddess of Ten Thousand Names".

The energy of the Triple Goddess is alive in the universe and inside of each woman. It is **transforming** energy; just as the seasons transform, so we transform and change from Maidens, to Mothers, to Crones, then back to Maidens again. In the wheel of the year the Crone of Samhain (Hallomas) becomes the Maiden of Spring Equinox.

Maiden, Mother and Crone represent time periods in a woman's life, but primarily are archetypal energies that also correspond to the phases of the New, Full and Dark Moons.

In *The Witches' Goddess,* The Goddess is described as a rainbow, with the colors representing Her three aspects: yellow and green for The Maiden, red and orange for The Mother, and blue, indigo and violet for The Crone.[4]

Jean Van Slyke

The Maiden, Maid or Nymph

At New Moon, The Crone aspect becomes the Maiden. Maiden energy is like that of springtime; new, hopeful and self-igniting. As the virgin (whole and centered in her own being), she exemplifies innocence, enchantment and new growth. She connects us to our power to act and take risks, and teaches us unself-consciousness, how to be carefree, and especially, how to be joyful. The Maiden's aura is the erotic spark of life and the freshness of the New Moon crescent.

Her youthful naivete feels no bounds or limitations as she takes risks and reaches out for life. The Maiden's lively spirit and curious mind capture the spirit of excitement and adventurousness. As an amazon and huntress she is assertive, self-reliant, courageous and strong.

Maiden Goddesses

Oya, Diana, Artemis, Bast, Persephone,
Eos, Renpet, Lada, Siduri

Colors: The pastel colors of spring.

The Mother

The Mother is the ripe, mature, powerful and full-blooded womon who brings healing to herself and those she nurtures. She is the fertile, sexual and sensuous adult who has learned to balance commitment and autonomy in her personal relationships. Through this aspect of ourselves we learn to reclaim our power and wholeness when we become intimate with another.

The Mother aspect manifests creativity, which is at its peak. She protects and nurtures all She has birthed, whether it be Her creations or Her beloved children, with a fierce passion that can seem merciless to those who do not understand the extent of Her love.

Her time is Full Moon when the energy is electric, magnetic and intense.

Mother Goddesses

Amaterasu, Juno, Tiamat, Parvati, Mawu, Demeter,
Hera, Freya, Copper Woman, Gaia,

Color: Red of womon's bloods and birthing.

The Crone or Hag

The source of all life lies in the dark womb of wimmin—**positive darkness** that is deep, warm and healing. As witches, we affirm and praise the darkness of our sisters' beautiful brown and black skin, our own dark wombs, our dark moon-time, and our Crone-selves. In relationship to womon's age, the Crone is at the end of her life. She is a womon alone, facing old age.

Her energy is letting go and travelling deep into our shadows, where we come face-to-face with problems, fears, angers and self-doubts. She gifts us with the power to release ourselves from defeating patterns that have ruled our lives.

"Crones are wise old womyn who have seen it all. They have compassion without the illusion or sentiment of youth. All knowledge of the Maiden and Mother live within her."[5] The Crone is the Teacher, the Hermit and the Cutter (see Chapter 3, Wimmin's Tarot #9 Life Card). This energy is about committed work on yourself, no matter what age you are, and the reclaiming of your power and wholeness. The Crone is a steadying influence on others and loves with calmness and understanding. After menopause we learn more about our Crone aspect, who is also our gateway to death. Then finally She guides us through the gate and points back to new beginnings as The Maiden.

The Crone represents the Dark Moon, a time of maximum soma lunar intensity.

Crone Goddesses

Erishkagel, White Buffalo Woman, Cerridwen, Hecate, Obatalla, Baubo, Holle, Baba Yaga, Sedna, Kali-Ma.

Colors: Maroon, Purple, Indigo Blue, Black.

THE ALTAR

Witches doing magic or a "working" generally use materials from the corporeal world to aid in focusing energy. It also feeds the senses and enhances ritual to have beautiful objects on which to feast our eyes. We place these objects on our altars.

The altar is a place for your deep self, a reflection of your internal landscape, and a home for the Goddess, inside and out. Altars vary immensely from woman to woman. Some are in a small box, some are built in walls, some are elaborate tables of round, square, and oblong shapes. Altars may appear on dashboards of cars, on outside decks, in crevices and crannies—anywhere you wish. The altar is **your** fantasy, so let your imagination run wild and express herself with freedom and abandon on your altar. Some women wish their altar to be "zen-like", free of clutter, with just a few beautiful, well-placed objects. Some may prefer their altar to contain a variety of objects and tools to use for magic. If your altar is below a window (like mine), a stained glass piece is beautiful hanging there.

Corners are wonderful opportunities with great potential. I have a large five-foot diameter half-round piece of wood, because the entire round took up too much space in my bedroom. It was also awkward to reach five feet back for other objects, or to light a candle on the back of the altar. My half-round is supported by a small short table with thick legs (as in a tarot reading, the Foundation is always important). In boxes under my altar I store all my candles, incense (mostly cedar and sage) and other supplies. On the top I place a vibrantly-colored handwoven cloth of blues and turquoises. My altar is a west altar (being a water sign, of course I created a west altar).

I believe the essential altar ingredients for doing magic are as follows. This can vary from one witch to another. Use your own judgement and do what works for you, not what someone tells you.

Three altar candles and a working candle are part of my basic setup: I use a white or lavender candle for the Maiden, a hot-pink, gold or red one for the Mother, and a blue or dark candle for the Crone. When I am doing a working—or a spell, as it is also called—I coordinate the color of the "working candle" with that of the chakra I am addressing.[6] For example, if I am doing a ritual for love or friendship I would use the heart-chakra color of green. If it is for my body or survival, I would use a red candle.

I first light the Maiden, Mother or Crone candle, depending on the phase of the moon. During the New Moon/Waxing phase, I burn a silver, or lavender candle for new beginnings, and on Full Moons a gold, red, or white candle, thanking the Goddess for her love and presence in my life. On Dark Moon I burn a purple, maroon or indigo candle for The Crone. Then I light a "working spell" candle.

Before lighting candles, I purify the altar and my body by smudging with cedar and/or sage, addressing the five directions, and clarifying my purpose. I always keep an image of the Goddess on the altar, and in season fresh flowers or herbs (sage and lavender fresh from my garden) as a reminder of Her growing influence. Sometimes a plant lives on the altar, and I have seen altars entirely comprised of hanging plants.

I feel it is important for the four elements to be present, (The Goddess image being the fifth. Water can be contained in a beautiful glass, metal, or pottery goblet or cup. I prefer to keep purified water in a colored glass container that I have charged in the light of the full moon. If you live where you don't get clean water out of the ground, buy distilled water or use ocean water and charge it with your energy. The fire element is represented by candles, a magic wand, or a ritual drum. Earth can be a variety of objects: rocks, crystals, stones, shells, pottery pieces, or a live plant   The air element is traditionally represented by an athame or witches knife, which should be made especially for you and magnetized. Other air element symbols are feathers, bird wings and bells. If you are fortunate enough to be safeguarding a bird's wing, it can be stored on your altar and then used in group rituals to fan the cedar, sage, and other kinds of incense. I don't use any of the "witches' incense" which is sold for specific purposes, although many women find them helpful. I don't like the smell of most incense and generally use cedar and sage that I have gathered in the desert. Cedar adds positive vibrations and sage banishes negativity. If you do use incense, you can obtain beautiful incense burners or other containers.

When I work my altar my intention is always clear, and I use my system of chakra candle-burning, that has proven successful time after time. I also keep a rattle on my altar, a symbol of the "blood rushing", just as the drum is the sound of the "heart beating".

During harvest time, vegetables, gourds, leaves and dried flowers are placed on the altar. Background music can help get you in the mood; in fact, an entire ritual can be based on music making.

Words of power affirm your spells. "So May It Be," "So Mote It Be," "So Be it," "Awomen," and "Of all the powers of three times three, this spell bound around shall be," are used frequently to intensify and bind what we say or chant. Also, when casting a spell you can tie a knot (either physically or in your imagination) that will bind its energies.

Group Altars

All women who come to the circle contribute something to the altar. One may bring the altar cloth, another the chalice, some bring candles and candleholders. If the group meets regularly it might wish to collect basic altar pieces to be used for rituals. One woman can be "Keeper of the Altar", making sure the ritual objects are present. The entire group can contribute flowers, gourds, or seasonal decorations. Different holydays inspire different altars, depending on the celebration. Please refer to Wheel of The Year section for seasonal correspondences.

KINDS OF RITUALS

Healing Ritual

At every Full Moon celebration I plan a time in the ritual for healing each other. However, if you, or a member of your ongoing circle is quite sick, you can call a circle in which all of the ritual energy goes to healing. Women needing healing do not have to be there, but it is useful. Following are some healing rituals you can use as guides.

Sending Healing to a Friend

Identify what chakra is involved. If your friend needs body healing, use a red candle, if she has a broken heart, use a green, heart chakra candle. Use the Chakra System of Candle-burning, which is in this chapter.

Purify your space with cedar and sage. Chant or raise energy for the ritual. Light your Maiden, Mother, Crone candles and your "working" candle (described under "Altars"). Visualize your friend and see her in an aura of glowing green light. See it radiating out of her body and circling around her.

Protection Ritual

You have come together because you, the group, or someone you love, is in danger. The purpose of this ritual is to protect them from harm.

When the energy is raised, the Priestess leads the group in a visualization where the Circle of Protection is invoked. You can use this circle of protection anytime it is needed, wherever you are. You can also use it to protect your house, car, or an animal. I first learned this from Womancraft Psychic Course, and I have taught the technique to women ever since.

Circle Of Protection

Visualize whatever you wish protected. I always surround myself, a friend, or my car with glowing rainbows, but you could also visualize a fence, a fog, dancing flowers, or loving arms; whatever feels protective to you is correct. The group repeats, "We now protect you (it, her, them) from all harm," and repeat this **three** times. Frequently throughout this writing, you will find that the repetition of words and chants is done three times. We do this in alignment with the threefold law of Wicce, referring to the Maiden, Mother, and Crone, the three aspects of the Goddess.

Singing Circle

The purpose of this circle is to sing your heart out. It can also be used as an emotional release, whereby a woman "sings" her feelings. Even though she may be making it up at the time, it has to be delivered in a singsong manner. There is **no** talking in the circle. The rattle is passed to the left and keeps going around until you have agreed to end.

Everyone makes a commitment to stay for the duration. This can be all night if you wish. Anyone can sing along with another woman, if it is a song they know. Obviously, when a woman is singing her feelings, it's not a good time to sing along; but this will be obvious, and you won't know the words anyway.

Respect should be given for equal time. If someone is taking up too much time when the rattle comes to her, the Priestess can intercede and gently tell the woman that her time is up. I am not advocating timing someone, but if respect is not being paid to equal time, this will have to be done. If you think you have taken a lot of time, compared to others, then make your turn shorter the next round, or pass the rattle. When you don't want to sing, or can't remember a song, you can pass the rattle though it is not customary to do that each time it comes to you. Everyone is at the ritual to sing, and if you keep passing, you become an observer, not a participator in the event.

Spell-Casting (Ritual of Creation)

Life presents us with problems and challenges. There are times when we want something s-o-o badly, or need something so much that we call a circle to ask others to help us manifest our needs by doing a spell. The entire energy and cone of power can be sent to create whatever is needed, and the words repeated, three times, "As We Say It, So Shall It Be". Alternatives to this are: "As We Create This, So Shall It Be", or "So Be It", or "So Mote It Be". These are called **The Words of Power,** and will be referred to as such for the remainder of this writing. The language is not so important as the intent. In fact, nothing you will intone, or do, is as important as the intent. If your intention is clear, strong, and pure, that is more powerful than any thing you might say or do, although your saying and doing carry out your intent. When you ask for something to happen, or visualize it, add "If the Goddess so wishes", or "If this be the best for the universe and for me".

Please don't do a ritual for someone else without their permission. This is manipulation. Always remember, whatever you do comes back to you three times. This is the threefold law— if you manipulate someone you will, at sometime in your future, be manipulated three times over. Whatever you do comes back to you threefold. This is a natural law of the universe and karma. In addition, if you do something really terrible to someone, you will have it come back ten times.

When spell-casting, the spell is repeated out loud, and visualized by the group. For example, if a womon is taking an exam of some kind, the situation surrounding the exam would be described. She would state all the reasons why she needs to pass this exam, then the chanting would begin and the cone of power sent to her to pass the exam. The womyn would visualize her walking out of the exam with a smile on her face, confident of success, and then later receiving her exam score, which would be a high grade. The group would then repreat the words of power three times. For a spell as short as this one, a special spell-casting circle would not be called, but the spell would be included in the regular workings of the circle. However, there are times when needs are great, and many wimmin in the group have requests for spells. If it is done as part of a full moon ritual or sabbat it would take all night, therefore a special ritual at a separate time to cast spells would be more appropriate.

Emotional Release

This type of ritual is done with a group to work out their feelings (in some cases differences) with each other. It can also be done with two or three wimmin. The circle is cast, the directions are addressed, and a candle is lit that represents clarity and peace. White or blue candles are good colors for this purpose. Emotional release is facilitated by passing the rattle, from womon to womon (in the case of only two, it would be passed back and forth), until resolution or release occurs (mutually agreed upon). Most women want to establish some kind of "ground rules" to define what is acceptable and what is not. This could be, for example, "no name-calling, no screaming", whatever is important to the womyn holding the ritual. The difference in this kind of circle and a singing circle is that talking, not singing, is the mode of communication for expressing emotion. Another helpful procedure is to wait one round of rattle-passing before responding to someone.

For example: I am participating in a two-woman emotional-clearing ritual and I have just told _____ (the woman I am processing with) that I have a lot of anger towards her for the way she walked out in the middle of our last argument. I am finished, and it is her turn with the rattle. Under the aforementioned agreement, she would not be able to respond to me until the next round; and would have to talk about something else this time. This is done to take the focus off responding to someone, rather than expressing your own feelings in the situation. Also, it gives the respondent time to "cool off" and listen, instead of immediately reacting by jumping in to dispute what the other womon has to say. This isn't something that would fit every occasion, but is a suggestion for situations where the participants are defensive. It is useful to have a mediator present, possibly a well-meaning, unbiased friend, making sure the ground rules are kept and things go smoothly, especially when the conflict has become deep and unresolvable.

The difference between this and other mediation techniques, is that The Goddess and the spiritual aspect of each woman is invoked. Beginnings and endings are conducted in the same way as other rituals.

Study Circle

A study circle is formed by a group of womyn wishing to learn more about Goddess lore, usually around Dark Moon. This gives a balance to the time the group meets on the Full Moon. Individual members of the group take responsibility for bringing topics to study. Sharing, conversation and singing are elements of a study circle. The circle can be opened and closed, as usual.

Notes - Chapter 1

1. Lee Laning & Vernette Hart, _Dreaming_ (MN:Word Weavers, 1983), p. 52.
2. Ibid., p. 16, (by Shekhinah Mountainwater).
3. Patrice Wynne, 'An Interview with Luisah Teish,' _Womanspirit Sourcebook_, (Harper and Row, 1988).
4. Janet and Stewart Farrar, _The Witches' Goddess_, (Washington: Phoenix Pub. Inc., 1987), pgs. 36-37.
5. Ibid, pg. 36.
6. See Chakra System of Candle Burning

Chapter 2
Elements of Ritual

CHAPTER 2 - ELEMENTS OF RITUAL

RITUAL PREPARATION

Ritual participants should discuss allergies to smoke, incense, perfume, etc. before any ritual is planned because there are some wimmin who become ill when they breathe them. It is with sisterhood and love that we omit certain items from our circle which oppress others and make them sick. One way of dealing with allergies to cedar and sage smoke is to smudge the ritual space beforehand, then let the smoke clear out before the ritual. If the ritual is to be done indoors, women can be smudged outside the door (weather permitting), and the allergic woman can stay removed from the proceedings. The smoke can then be extinguished before she approaches the door. There are also other ways to purify the ritual space. Many groups sprinkle salt or salt water for purification, omitting smudging altogether.

It is interesting and helpful for everyone involved to do some amount of research for the Sabbat or Esbat (full moon) that is being celebrated. This way our knowledge grows. There are many feminist ceremonial/ritual books available now, so expand yourself by studying rituals that have been done by others and bringing things you like about them to your circle, as well as creating new things to do.

It is wonderful to have rituals recorded so that you may use them, or parts of them, at some future time. Or you may choose to pass them on to other groups. Although the reason may not be obvious at the time, it is valuable to have a written record. I would not be writing sections of this book if I hadn't recorded my rituals.

Before you proceed, decide which kind of ritual you are going to have, and then plan it.

Creating Sacred Space

There is no **one way** to do a ritual or to create magic. Before you begin, spend 15-30 minutes together to check in with each other and discuss what you will do.

If you are doing a solitary ritual the time can be much shorter, say 5-15 minutes to meditate and center yourself before you begin.

I will proceed with this material as if for a group ritual. If you wish to work alone at your altar, please adapt it.

The first step is to decide on a space, outside or inside, under a tree, around a firepit, beside the water, or in an open field. If this is to be an outdoor circle around a firepit, the hole has to be dug and a large space around the fire is cleared for fire protection. Larger rocks are then put in a circle around the fire hole. Firewood is gathered and stacked, and the fire set with matches readily available for lighting. This can take a lot of time, and one or two "firewomyn" usually volunteer to do this work. They are also responsible for keeping the fire burning during the entire ritual without distracting the womyn or disrupting the energy. If you've never done this job before, or do not have a woodstove in your home, it would be a good idea to get some lessons from an experienced firewomon before you take on the task. (At least one of the firewomyn should be experienced.)

To make a smaller, more manageable flame, many witches place an iron cauldron in the middle of the circle and light a fire in it. The cauldron can also be used outside when there is fire danger instead of a larger fire that sends sparks into the air. Cauldrons on stands are used inside, as long as the fire is kept low and precaution is taken. You can open the door of a wood-burning stove which can take up one section of the circle, with the firewomyn sitting on each side tending it; the rest of the circle forms around them.

The most common setup for indoor work, when weather does not permit outside rituals, is the use of candles in the center of the circle. Some groups prefer that each woman bring her own candleholder and candle to set in front of her, and Maiden, Mother, and Crone group candles are placed on the altar. Differently colored candles are associated with the seasons.

It is important to have a short planning meeting, if possible, a week or so before the ritual, or tasks can be agreed upon over the telephone with members of the group. If you belong to an ongoing group, this can be decided at a previous meeting. If you have a rotating Priestess, sometimes called "The Roadwoman", this definitely has to be decided beforehand, as she is responsible for a great many things in coordinating the ritual. If there are unassigned tasks or circle positions (such as who will address the directions), the Priestess will have to contact others who are willing to do this. If you have a womon who has been selected unanimously as The Priestess (some womyn call her High Priestess), this is not a problem. It is increasingly common in feminist covens that the Priestess be a rotating responsibility. I say "responsibility", rather than "privilege", because I feel it is a difficult job requiring a lot of energy and commitment. Whether or not the Priestess and other wimmin who agree to take responsibility have done their preliminary planning can be the most important factor in the success of the ritual.

In feminist groups there is a sentiment against leadership, which is on one hand, positive, and on the other, a hindrance. Feminists do not like **anyone** to tell us what to do. This is a given. Most of us have had (and still have, in our jobs) someone constantly telling us what to do, and we are tired of it. Therefore, there is a tendency to come to a ritual and just hope it comes out right. No one wants a leader, everyone is a leader. Right? Wrong. I have suffered through so many unplanned circles without a leader and been miserable. No one knows what to do, no one has done any homework, and no one wants to be pushy and try to lead the circle. So everyone flounders around. I am not saying this always happens, but it has happened too frequently for me to feel good about going to a ritual where there is no circle leader and no plan. If a group has been meeting for a long time and has organically developed a general plan that each ritual follows, and the wimmin know exactly what they are doing and are used to each other, then that is a different situation. Rituals with different participants each time, and no set plan can be a disaster.

Structure can be beneficial if it does not become solidified. Leadership, and the power that goes with it, can be beneficial if the power is passed, meaning passed from one to another, so that the ones who have the power do not always keep it. If a group has chosen one woman to be their Priestess, they are saying they are willing to take a chance that this one woman can handle the power, and that they do not yet wish to have it. I believe that if someone is the Priestess, she should always be willing to give up her position to another capable womon who might want it—be that for a night or a year. She should ask each time if there is a womon present who wishes to take the Priestess position at the next circle.

From experience, I can truthfully say that there are very few women who want to perform Priestess duties. Many women feel they are too inexperienced; many think they won't be good at it. I always encourage wimmin to try. It's a big risk, but spiritually we should be willing to take risks for our growth. If you are one of these women, remember that every Priestess was once in your shoes and she was at one time a beginner. The best way to learn is by doing. I don't mean come to one circle and then jump in and volunteer to be Priestess. There is a time to learn and a time to take power. You must go through the learning period which is generally agreed to be a minimum of a year and a day of concentrated study. If you have been coming to ritual say, five years, and have never been the Priestess, you might try to search your soul to see if you are ready for it. There will always be some womon who will never want the Priestess job, for whatever reasons. That is alright, too. Each womon helps create a ritual by giving her energy and participating.

Excessive wordiness in a ritual can be a problem. There should be a balance between things said and things done. Music is also important and should never be omitted. Group participation in womyn's spirituality is an important aspect and every ritual should be structured to include this. As your group becomes familiar with each other, there should be several openings for spontaneity in words and action. Passing the rattle is a good way to get this going within a structured framework. For improvising your rituals you may also experience a need for some kind of signal that means, "Let's get on with it" when the energy drags. This could be a sound, a gong, or a chant that the Priestess initiates to give this signal.

Another kind of preparation for a ritual or circle is the idea of fasting for a period of time (half a day, one day, a few days, a week) to increase your psychic sensitivity. Fasting, done with moderation and caution, cleans out the physical body and prepares us psychically for magical work. In many cases, fasting requires solitude and rest, an excellent preparation for any ritual situation.

Preparing food for the feast that takes place after the ritual is another way we give and create. If circle members celebrate with dinner before the circle you will most likely be sluggish or fall asleep because food slows down your system. I have been to many circles where a potluck took place **before** the ritual. I am convinced this does not work. I have seen it over and over again. Wimmin wonder why their rituals don't work. One of the biggest reasons is eating substantial amounts beforehand. It is wonderful to be able to feast **after** the circle because psychic work makes you very hungry. It's great to have that wonderful food to dive into. If you **must** eat before a ritual, it is best to eat lightly so you are not weighted down when you want to fly.

Expectation

The most important element in ritual is, I believe, the element of expectation and anticipation. This involves self-preparation in order to get the most out of the experience of magic. If you are going to a ritual, try to do very little the rest of the day (if you can). If you can't take a few hours, take as much time as possible to prepare yourself psychically and physically. If the flowers are blooming, take a walk and pick fresh flowers for the altar. If it's raining, meditate or listen to some music that will open up your channels. Give the day to yourself and to the Goddess. She deserves it just as you do. If you don't have to work that day, give yourself this time to think about the holiday you are celebrating, and what it means to you in particular, and to the planet. Have a bath, do tai chi or yoga, or take a long time to pick out your ritual dress, adorn yourself and gather things you will need. Prepare a dance, a poem, anything that you want to share with others.

Make this day an experience to remember, a time out of time. This is the essence of ritual, giving this spiritual, ritualistic part of your life **equal time** with the other, more rational aspects of existence. We seldom do this for ourselves. If it is easier to keep promises to others than to yourself, promise the Goddess that you will celebrate all Her holydays in this way (or all Her full moons, or whatever promise you wish). And keep that promise. You give to Her, you give to Yourself, for She is You and You are She. "Maiden, Mother, Crone in Me, all three in harmony," sings Shekhinah Mountainwater. This is **your** time and **your** life. You can make it anything you wish.

This all connects with the element of expectation. If you follow these guidelines you are creating an expectation. Who would spend the whole day getting ready for some event of little importance? By preparing, you are creating the expectation of a great happening. Expectation is the bare bones of the craft: it's creating reality; you expect something to happen. Creating reality is imagining it (visualization) and **expecting it to happen**. A feeling of magic will grow out of it. By dressing and bathing yourself you will begin to feel important and loved. By taking the time to plan and create something to share with others during the ritual (for example, reading a story you love), **you are creating the ritual.** By gathering flowers, you are **creating sacred space**. That is why you have been out there digging up the earth for the firepit, chopping the wood, clearing the ground; you are creating sacred space for the circle. In taking time to lovingly prepare food for the feast, you are giving of your energies to yourself and the others. You are **expecting** an important event.

Visualize this scenario: Sally gets up on the day of the circle. It is Saturday, so she knows she has a million things to do. She grabs a cup of coffee, runs out of the house with her laundry, drives to the laundromat, does her laundry, then decides to get some lunch. She stands in line at a fastfood restaurant, eats her food on the way to the store to buy something new to wear (she wants to look good because there's a womon there who she's interested in). She shops, can't find anything she likes, so she decides to run around and do a few more errands. After all, she's got an hour left in her schedule! By the time Sally gets home, it's time to eat dinner. She sits down to a big meal, gets dressed, and rushes out the door.

When she gets to the ritual she apologizes for being 20 minutes late (she notices they have been waiting for her). She tells the group she was late because she had to have dinner. They tell her there's a potluck afterwards—she has forgotten that. She didn't take the time to prepare anything to share, like a story, a dance, or song—so she feels left out and has a terrible time. She's not hungry at the feast afterwards and she almost fell asleep during the circle. She wonders why she even bothers with these circles! Besides, the wombon she wants to see isn't here anyway! What's wrong??

We all have choices, no matter what excuses we can rationalize for why we did or didn't do something. We can choose to give ourselves the time to prepare for a magical experience. It's all what **you** make it. The Priestess might do her job, but she's not going to create it for you. The rest of the group can be loving and supportive and give of themselves, but only you can give yourself the magic, the expectation and the anticipation. **Gift** yourself the time for magic. The circle is not where we go to be entertained by others. They are part of it, but each womoon must be responsible for the success of any ritual.

Surrendering Your Resistance

The single most important element for a successful ritual is the element of surrender. For some wimmin this is not a problem and for others it can be a gigantic block keeping her from feeling the magic. There are a variety of resistances to overcome.

One of these is bringing small children, who have no desire to participate in a ritual circle. Children are an important part of life, and there are some very special children who **want** to be at ritual, and can participate and add to it. However, these children are few and far between. When children are very young they usually can't sit still, or they make a fuss because Mommy is doing something else. Some children come to ritual and sleep, absorbing the magic in their dreams. Sometimes it works well, but I have also been to many circles where women have brought their children because they don't want to get a babysitter. If there are women with children in an ongoing group and they need childcare in order to come to rituals, the women can take up a collection before the circle begins. The mother should state how much she needs and everyone can contribute. The Goddess always watches over and makes sure enough is collected.

I am definitely **not** suggesting that any woman who brings her child to a ritual is doing so because of resistance. This is not always the case. If you think your young child can fit in and be a part of the ritual or go peacefully to sleep, by all means bring her, but if there is **any** possibility she will disrupt the energy, leave her at home. As for older children, if a mother asks me about this, I always reply, "If you think your child wants to come **for herself**, to experience the ritual, by all means bring her, but if she is coming because you want her to come, that's the wrong reason." Many older girls have a personal desire to be in circle; this has always worked out to be a wonderful experience for everyone.

Another resistance I have encountered over the years is that in very rare instances a woman will come drunk because she is an alcoholic and she is afraid of magic. This is always a disruption of the energy. Now most rituals are alcohol-free and juice is passed instead of wine, but some circles prefer to pass a glass of wine for libations.

One of the most obvious resistances that I have encoutered at ritual is when wimmin who **talk in the middle of a ritual.** I am always horrified when this happens because it interrupts the magical energy and brings us back to ordinary, everyday reality. We are in the circle to transform this world as we know it. Between the worlds you don't chatter about everyday matters. Talking of these things is unecessary and disrupting. When we come into circle and the Priestess declares that we are between the worlds, try to be there. It is also rude to talk with a friend during a ritual, as it excludes and distracts everyone.

A word should be said here addressing the concept of "the veil between the worlds". This is a metaphor to describe the place that exists between the world of the dead and the world of the living. This world "in between" is a magical world, a place out of time.

Overcoming Resistance

Ways of overcoming resistance and opening yourself to The Goddess:

Chanting - This breaks down resistance quite nicely and is a magical journey inside yourself.

Naming - One of the other most effective paths to breaking resistance is to name yourself a witch. In the early days of feminist witchcraft it was suggested to repeat to yourself three times, **"I am a Witch"**. By naming our reality, we create it. This worked very well for me, as once I said it, I believed it and acted upon it.

Action - Jumping in and doing magic, taking a chance, a leap of faith, diving in, head first. Often, action is the only antidote to resistance.

Studying - If something is unfamiliar to you, or frightening, obtaining knowledge about it will disperse the fear. Then you know generally what's going to happen.

Watching - If you are insecure about being at a ritual, go to it anyway, and keep your participation to a minimum until things are familiar to you. Watch others, be silent, pass the rattle if you feel insecure. Women are compassionate and sensitive. Everyone has been in your shoes at one time or another.

Trust - Trust in the Goddess that she will show you the way. Ask for help with your resistances. Opening up can sometimes be a slow process that takes time. Trust yourself, that you can grow and change.

There are three basic modes of ritual: Private (often called "practising solo", or "solitary"), a coven, and an open group (called a grove). I have done all three. I have been part of a coven that was closed except for particular holy days, been part of one that was not open for anyone but members at any time, and I do private rituals on an ongoing basis. For most of my time in the craft I have been part of open groups with a few core members.

A community ritual involves the entire community, such as a trysting (pagan marriage) ritual, and can involve others who do not consider themselves pagans or witches.

Ritual Dress

This is an aspect of ritual that most women neglect. The circle is a place where you go **between** the worlds, which means that you go to a place of magic that is different from our ordinary lives. It is not a place of spirit where we die or lose our bodies. Between the worlds is a place out of time. If you've ever been to a ritual that was stimulating and wonderful, you know that you forgot about time there. When the ritual was over it seemed quite short, but several hours had gone by. We need help to get between the worlds, to get out of mundane reality, and our bodies and thoughts that are very much of this world (too much of the time, I feel). Magical help can come in many forms: music, psychic trance, a suspension of "ordinary" actions and beliefs. Ritual dress is one of these helpers to get "out of ourselves". It serves the purpose of disguise. Since we are stuck in this reality, we need to trick ourselves into moving into another dimension.

The world you are entering is a world of magic, and the talking you do there is talking about the magic, and what you are experiencing in creating it. The ritual dress disguises you to yourself and others. Doing magic involves taking risks. It is sometimes easier to take these risks if you are someone else, or at least, another quite outrageous aspect of yourself. My advice is to always be as outrageous as you can when you dress for a ritual. The more outrageous, the better. Do it! Don't be shy. If everyone agrees to do it, then you don't have to be afraid to be the only one.

Purification

Purify the ritual space by smudging each womon with sage and cedar. One of the wombon in the group can volunteer to be "cedar woman". This job is to make sure cedar and sage are brought to the circle, and that at the beginning each woman's aura is smudged with smoke from both plants. Cedar woman starts with the Priestess, or Roadwoman, and moves to the left. She lights the cedar and blows on it to put out the flame. The cedar should still be smoking in a container (such as an ashtray, smudge pot, or sea shell). She then fans the smoking herb around the entire aura of the Priestess, who stands with hands open, facing up, opening herself to the smudging. If the smoking stops, the cedar has to be re-lit and blown out so the smoke is rekindled. Another way is to pass the smoking herbs to each other, taking turns smudging.

Some women prefer to use incense for this, and others prefer to walk to the left, on the outer perimeters of the circle, scattering salt or salt water. Whatever you do, it is not so much **what** you do, as the **intent** of what you do. If you have the intent then no matter what you do, it is correct.

MAIN BODY OF THE RITUAL

Beginnings

Each wimmin's spirit group or coven casts their circle and welcomes the members in different ways. In some rituals, a pentacle is drawn on the wimmin's foreheads with aromatic oil. The Mother River Spirit group paints black moons on their foreheads at Dark Moon and white moons at Full Moon.

One beginning is to go around and each say a prayer with the prayer-smoke ritual. Prayer smoke is adapted from Native American peyote ritual and is done by passing a pipe of mullein herb, which is lit by each woman. Mullein is the only smoke that helps heal the lungs. Usually the pipe that is used is a long-stemmed pipe used only for these occasions. The woman lights the pipe and says a prayer—for herself, for a loved one, for the group, or for the earth. She then passes it to the left, until everyone has finished. If you do not wish to smoke the mullein, just hold the pipe while you say your prayer. If you do not wish to share your prayer but wish to smoke, do that. You may also choose to do neither.

Openings are a good time to sing songs and raise energy, or you may prefer to dance, or tell stories. Another rite for beginning a ritual is to do healings

This is the point where I prefer to begin the drum. The Priestess may begin the drumming and later pass it to someone else, or the drum may be passed around the circle. The herstory of the celebration can be given now. Stories are read, experiences are shared, everyone shares their knowledge of information they have researched before the circle. For example: if this is Samhain (pronounced "Sow-in"), lore would be spoken of what this holyday means, traditionally and to contemporary witches. The entire group would contribute and the appointed "scribe" or "recorder" of the circle would add to her written knowledge at this time.

Casting the Circle

This is done in a variety of ways. In traditional Wicce the High Priestess casts the circle with a sword, admitting the members one by one. On the altar is a bowl of salt, of water, and three candles. There are also candles in each of the four corners. She then names three wimmin. One carries a bowl of saltwater, (which has been ritually combined), around the circle parameters to the left (doesil), sprinkling saltwater as she goes. The next womoon carries the smoking incense censer in the same way. The last woman carries an altar candle, placing it back on the altar when she is done. The directions are then addressed.

In feminist Dianic Wicce the circle is cast in a variety of ways, as is fitting the eclectic nature of women's spirituality. It can be done with salt water, incense, candles (as described above), a ritual wand, flowers, or an athame (witch's knife) and is done to the left for **invoking**.

The Priestess declares the circle is opened, that we are now "between the worlds". This means that whatever happens in this sacred space is done in a spirit that reflects out-of-ordinary-reality. Everyone will have taken care of body functions before the circle is cast, and "ordinary talk" is suspended until the ritual is over.

In dire circumstances an opening can be traced with a wand or athame for a woman to temporarily leave, and it is ritually closed again on her return.

Openings

You are about to enter
A vortex of power
A place beyond imagining
Where birth and death
Dark and light
Joy and pain meet.
You are about to step between
the worlds
Beyond time, outside the realm
Of your human life.

Ritual for Opening and Closing[3]

To open the circle, the ritual area is smudged. The wimmin arrange themselves in order of age, from the oldest to the youngest. The two oldest womyn begin the ritual. They hold hands, facing each other. The next-oldest approaches and they raise up their hands to let her enter between their arms (diagram, next page). They look her in the eye and say, in unison:

**"From women you are born into this world,
From women you are born into this circle."**

This can turn into a raucous time-consuming rite if there are many women involved. Women participating should be aware of those waiting, and the fact that there is a ritual that will follow. Do this ritual opening with respect for time.

They then simultaneously kiss her on the cheeks. Then after a brief pause (seconds), they raise up their arms, and the woman exits their womb-like embrace and stands next to them. The next woman approaches and the procedure is repeated. When she exits, she makes a twosome with the one waiting woman and the next-oldest passes through two sets of two women, and so on. The number of twosomes increases as the ritual proceeds, and at last there are many bridges of arms. The two eldest make their way through the labyrinth to the end. The words and cheek kisses are repeated by each set of women in the line, so if you begin at the end of the line you will go through many hands and arms before you reach the end.

When the two eldest have gone through the chain of kisses, they end up holding hands at the end, just as they started. At this point everyone drops their hands to their sides and takes the hand of the woman beside her, instead of across from her. Thus, the circle is formed and proceeds as usual—beginning with addressing the directions.

At the end of the entire ritual, the process of entering the circle is repeated in reverse, for closing, the youngest to the eldest. The words repeated are somewhat different:

**"From women you are born into this circle,
From women you are born into this world."**

Passing the Rattle

The rattle is passed and the womon who holds the rattle holds the power. She can ask the group to participate in anything she wishes (within reason, of course). Many womon come to ritual with strong plans and desires: a spiral dance, an African dance (be sure to provide music for this), a guided meditation, the reading of a poem, the playing of an instrument, asking the group to participate in a short play of some kind — the options are infinite.

Raising the Cone of Power

The most effective way to do this is by chanting. It can also be done with drumming, dancing *the spiral dance*, and prayer. The cone of power can be sent to energize spells: for example, a circle of protection, a money spell, etc.

I like to chant the word **Ma.** It has the same universal sound as **Om,** and it is female. When womyn first begin to chant **Ma** we often get in touch with deep feelings connected with the word, feelings that bring up scenes of one's mother, of oneself as a mother, and of the Earth, our Mother, who is in such pain right now.

RAISING ENERGY
by Norma Joyce

Feel yourself..... feel the energy building in you..... feel the energy coming in your right hand from your sister..... feel it moving out through your left to your sister on that side..... feel your energy moving through the circle..... and as you feel it move you feel it moving down into the Earth..... down into the Mother..... you feel Her beat..... the pulsing of Her heartbeat..... and as you feel that energy, feel also the roots of your being going down and joining Her....going down....going down....until you feel the total connection....feel grounded and know that any work you do....any letting go....you will still be centered and grounded in the Earth....you are protected by Her being....stay grounded in Her and bring your awareness of the energy up into the center of your being....feel your continuing connection with the Mother and your connection with your circle of sisters....all adding to the energy that you are creating....that you are raising....feel now that you are able to let go....the cares of the day.....the concerns that tie you to your problems....the addictions that keep us from growing into Goddess energy....let go and feel yourself soaring to the universe....go out there....leave your troubles behind and become one with all....you are now in the place of the over-soul....the place where your questions and answers have their beginnings and endings..... sense now the questions you have and allow the Goddess energy of your higher self answer....ask as many as you want....you have the answers....let go and soar with the Goddess....

As you have let go, feel Her potential within you....feel Her energy and yours becoming one....and the energy rises in the circle as all become one....building and building the energy....and we build it even stronger as we join together with....(whatever chant the Priestess wants, she starts it off and welcomes any other chants to follow)....allow the Goddess energy and the energy we have raised with our voices continue to climb as we get ready to send it....feel it climbing higher and higher....becoming stronger and stronger....more and more contained....build it now for (whatever your purpose, for a person(s), etc.) and let it go....send it off. The Goddess is alive.

GROUNDING AND RUNNING ENERGY

Sit or stand in a comfortable, quiet place, although you can do this anywhere to be grounded, even on a noisy and busy city street. Plant your feet solidly on the earth. If this is not possible, try for a wood floor. Relax, quiet your mind, and begin to breathe deeply. Follow your breath into your body and out again. Open up the bottoms of your feet by imagining two little doors that you can open or close at will. When you feel your foot chakras open wide, slowly begin to pull up energy from Mother Earth. She has an infinite supply of love and healing that's easy to draw into you, and She shares it freely. Mentally check to see if you are still breathing deeply, and if your foot doors are still open. Again, draw the energy up your legs and into your body, over and over.

Ground yourself with a cord as wide as your body or aura, and create an energy path. Visualize whatever kind of cord you wish, coming out of your lower spine at your tailbone, going down deep into the earth on the energy path you have just created, down through your feet, into the mud, through the water table and bedrock, and then down into the molten fire at the center of the earth, a fire that energizes and rebirths. Don't censor what you visualize for a grounding cord, just let it form on its own. Whatever comes to you is alright. Some women visualize snakey, glittering cords, some have thick rope-like umbilical cords, some have beaver tails, ribbons. Trust whatever you create, no matter how foolish it may seem at the time. What your old wise womonself senses is good. Breathe deep, relax and focus on your body.

This entire process should take about 3-5 minutes. It is a preparation for chanting, but also a preparation for any kind of psychic work or magic. Doing it in a circle with others strengthens its power. Before any ritual is closed the Priestess should ground with the group.

CHANTING

When I began to organize and lead womyn's spiritual circles, I didn't know the mechanics of chanting very well. Shekhinah Mountainwater helped me learn and showed me how to be a better Priestess and Witch. She saw my potential, drew it out, praised it and nurtured it, so I could advance rapidly in my development. I will share with you my method of chanting.

For groups: Form a circle and hold hands. Your left hand is up for receiving energy, and your right hand is down for giving energy.

Now you are ready to chant.

Begin by humming, first with your mouth closed, so that the hum becomes a vibrating buzzing in your head, charging and cleaning your inner body. After doing this for a moment or so, open your mouth and let the sound out, projecting it into the center of the circle where it can meet the voices of all the others. (If you are doing this alone, it will be different.) **Everyone should not begin at the same time,** but you should start a few seconds after the woman on your right begins. Sound, like anything else in the circle, goes clockwise around to the **left, doesil,** (except when ending a circle, or undoing a spell, it goes to the **right,** (called **widdershins**). This creates layers of sound which do not end before the chant ends. Just as one womon is ending her breath, another is in the middle of hers, and still another is just beginning.

Sound will meet in the middle of the circle and a "buzzing" will begin. This is the **Cone of Power,** the **Spiral** of energy that builds stronger and deeper, reaching a crescendo, until it is spent. When the cone has reached its peak, the Priestess calls for it to be released and sent out to a person or the universe for whatever purpose has been designated beforehand. Names of friends/loved ones in need are called out at this time. If the chant has been initiated as part of a spell to create positive energy, its purpose is stated out loud before the chant. Chanting can last for 5 minutes or 45, depending on the energies of those involved.

You can also chant by yourself if you wish. This is a wonderful tool for self-knowledge and personal transformation. Follow the same method.

I chant **"Ma"**, for the Mother. The use of **"Ma"** by feminist witches is something that has increased in the past few years. Fifteen years ago when we were first chanting **'Ma'** it was virtually unknown. You can also chant particular Goddess' names such as **D-i-a-n-a,** or **H-e-c-a-t-e.** I have included a list of Goddess names to be used for different Full Moons, Solstices, Equinoxes and Holydays. When you first begin to chant **Ma,** deep, painful feelings can arise. It might remind you of your mother, or grandmother, or a child. This will pass.

New Moon Circles - Chant Diana or other New Moon or Maiden Goddesses. Some Maiden Goddess names that we have chanted are: Lada, Hina, Artemis, Calafia, or Mami Watu (The Mermaid), Persephone, and Kore.

Full Moon Circles - Chant names of Mother Goddesses associated with the moon in her fullness. We chant, "Yemaya" every Full Moon. She is the Yoruban Goddess of the Full Moon and the ocean. We also chant Luna, Demeter, Mawu, Innana, and other Mother Goddesses.

Dark Moon Circles - There are many powerful and healing Crone Goddesses of the Darkness. Some of her names are: Hecate, Kali, Grey Mare, Ix Chel, Cerridwen, Buffalo Womon, and Lilith.

Sometimes we chant names of the womyn in the circle, also names of our mothers and grandmothers. Remembering our dead on Samhain (also called Hallomas) gives us the opportunity to contact our mothers, grandmothers, and loved ones who have gone to the spirit world.

In order to accomplish the chanting of a variety of Goddess names smoothly, one woman will begin by calling out the name of a Goddess, then slowly begin to chant that name. When someone else (or the same womon) wishes to change the name, she calls out the name of another Goddess and everyone begins to chant that name.

In ritual work, timing is of the utmost importance. When the group is enthralled in the climactic joy of chanting one Goddess' name, it is not the time to jump in with a new name. Wait until the energy is waning to start another chant. However, if you have a name in mind, don't wait until the chant has almost died and the energy is too low to present your offering. Perhaps the reason no one has begun to chant another name is because no one can think of one, or the group has been so involved in the ecstasy of the moment that it hasn't occurred to anyone. There is a natural psychic end to the chants that you will learn to recognize over time. If the Priestess has ceased to participate in the chanting, you can assume that she is gently leading the group out of this activity and into another phase of the ritual.

Anything goes—there are no rules and regulations to magic. Some things "work" better than others, or feel more comfortable. Experiment, make up your own chanting rituals. There is a great reservoir of power in chanting, one which we can draw into us for magic and healing. For purposes of chanting, I include the attributes of the elements and four directions:

Element of Air and the East

Chanting for mental strength, clarity, communication, decisionmaking, studying and peace of mind. For Goddess names to chant for the above purposes and on Full Moons in Aquarius, Libra, and Gemini see The East, p. 44.

Element of Fire and the South

Chanting for energy, taking action. (For example, in a Take Back the Night March it would be wonderful to chant Calafia and Cerridwen.) For Goddess names to chant on Full Moons in Aries, Leo, Sagittarius, see direction of The South, p. 47.

Element of Water and the West

Chanting to heal the emotions, love, compassion, intensity, psychic ability. For Goddess names to chant on Full Moons in Scorpio, Pisces, and Cancer, see direction of The West, p. 50.

Element of the Earth and the North

For grounding, material matters, work, money, body, survival. For Goddess names to chant on Full Moons in Virgo, Taurus and Capricorn see direction of The North, p. 53.

Some chants to use for rituals are as follows:

**Blessed Be, Blessed Be
The Transformation of Energy (repeat and repeat)**

"We are the flow, we are the ebb,
we are the weavers, we are the web,

We are the weavers, we are the web,
We are the witches back from the dead...

We are the witches back from the dead,
we are the weavers, we are the web"
Shekhinah Mountainwater

There is a method of quickly inducing trance state while chanting, which I also learned from Shekhinah Mountainwater, called "Stirring The Cauldron". It is performed like this: move your upper body (from the waist up) in a circle to the left. You might have to close your eyes as this can make you dizzy. Imagine you are stirring a large cauldron with your body as the soup-spoon. This is done during chanting, or any time you need to move into a trance state. Try it first sitting down, then standing.

ENDING THE RITUAL

After spells, the rattle can be passed again and again, until the energy is at a peak and magic is felt so strongly in the room that it feels like electricity zapping back and forth among the women.

When she intuits it is time, the Priestess will begin to wind down the energy by grounding the circle . This can be done by a guided visualization, or in the case of experienced participants, the suggestion can b e made that everyone ground herself.

BANISHING THE CIRCLE

To banish the circle, the energy is grounded, the directions are thanked and appreciated, in reverse order; Center, North, West, South, East. The Priestess chants, "The circle is open, but never broken". Then she leads the group in the song "Merry meet and merry part, and merry meet again", repeated three times.

May the circle be open, but never broken
May the peace of The Goddess go in our hearts
Merry meet and merry part
And merry meet again

Plan your celebration to take into account your needs and desires. This is a suggested basic plan for structure, in case some of the womyn are new to ritual and are at a loss as to what to do. You can use this ritual outline time and time again, adding and deleting whatever is needed at any particular time.

INSTRUCTIONS FOR THE SPIRAL DANCE

Hold hands, all facing the same direction. The leader starts walking, as if to form a circle, as large as the room permits, with all wimmin following.

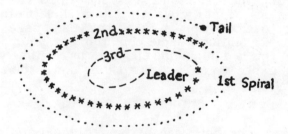

When she meets the tail of the spiral (* in diagram), she passes it and moves inside, creating another inner circle (indicated at its beginning by small stars).

After this inner spiral (circle) is complete, she continues spiralling inward one more time (dashes on diagram) to create still a third circle. This will probably be only a few paces, depending on the size of the circle. Instead of completing this last circle, the leader turns back, almost 180 degrees, and leads the spiral in the opposite direction, spiralling outward. Now, the womon on the tail will be facing her, but moving in the opposite direction. After she has made three outward spirals, she begins the inward spiral again on the outside of the tail.

THE CHAKRA SYSTEM OF CANDLE BURNING

I was intuitively drawn to creating and using this system of candle-burning. It was a logical conclusion to my work with the chakra system in creating Magical Crystals and Magical Pyramids. Since each chakra (energy center of the body) represents a different energy, it seemed fitting to use that chakra color for healing and for creating realities that corresponded to her energy. For example, the first chakra represents **survival** and the representative color is **red**. I do money rituals burning a **red** candle because money is a **survival** issue. Another example of using a red candle for first-chakra needs is when my friend had a serious operation. She asked me to do a ritual for her at the exact time of her operation: I did, and burned a **red** candle for her physical well-being and **survival**. as the first chakra is also related to the physical body. Once I began using this system I was so amazed with the results that I have abandoned all other candle/color systems. This is not to say that other systems do not work well: but that this works best for me.

Chakra Self-Blessing

Prepare a chalice of sea water. Dip your fingers in it and touch each part of your body as you bless yourself.

Bless me, Goddess, for I am your child.

Visualize Purple: Bless my mind, clear as the mountain air that I may always remember your wisdom and magnificence.

Visualize Indigo: Bless my eyes, flashing with the passion of life, that I may always see myself and others clearly. Bless my ears, that I may always hear your music.

Visualize Sky Blue or Turquoise: Bless my mouth, to bring forth laughter. May I always taste your nectar and sing your praises.

Visualize Green: Bless my heart, full of love, joy and compassion. May I always remember love for all creatures.

Visualize Yellow: Bless my breasts and belly, abundant and full. May I always nurture my sisters and myself.

Visualize Orange: Bless and heal my yoni and sex, open and flowing. May I always know the power of passion.

Visualize Red: Bless my hands, gentle and healing. May I always do your work. Bless my bowels, that I may eliminate that which I do not need. Bless my legs and feet. May I always walk gently on the earth in the paths of my courageous foremothers.

Thank you, Goddess for your protection and love.

This blessing can also be done for another (substitute "your" for "my"). In blessing each other we share our collective love for the Goddess.

CALLING THE FIVE DIRECTIONS

The Guardians or Goddesses of each direction open the gateways between the worlds. Five womyn are choosen for this before the circle. One woman can do two or more directions, or the Priestess can do all the directions. The East is the first direction to be invoked. All women face The East. You may wish to raise both your hands, palms facing that direction, or you may wish to make the sign of the sacred yoni, which involves touching your index fingers together with thumbs touching. This is also the position of the hands for Drawing Down the Moon (see diagram, Chapter 5).

The wombon who will call The East chants, "Guardians (Goddesses) of The East, bring your winds of change, your words, songs and breaths, to this circle, join us tonight", or she can also call on the Goddesses of The East by name. She may wish to shake the rattle, ring a bell or beat the drum while she addresses the direction. After she is done, the womyn can repeat "Blessed Be" if they wish.

The circle now faces The South and the procedure is repeated, using words, Goddesses, and prayers to The South, then to the West, The North and The Center. When the ritual is over, the Guardians (Goddesses) are thanked in reverse order: Center, North, West, South, East.

Be passionate and innovative in your callings and thankings. Listen to other wimmin's poetic invocations of the directions and draw from your own ritual experiences to give you some ideas. This is a time to be creative, don't always intone standard phrases from what has been written by others. Make up new and innovative things to say and do when calling The Directions.

THE FIVE ELEMENTS AND FIVE DIRECTIONS

As I mentioned previously in the section on "Altar", I make sure the five elements are always represented in material form on the altar. In The Craft we begin by calling the five elements, each having a particular direction of air, earth, fire, water, and spirit (familiar four cardinal points of the compass, the fifth being the center) to cast the circle and create sacred space. We invoke these elements to bring us to a place removed from our daily reality, inviting their guidance, power and wisdom. Throughout time the Directions have been a symbol that wimmin have used to describe our relationship and gratitude to Her living body, the Earth, the basis of our earth-based spirituality. They form a system of correspondences in which we can associate each direction with an element, certain personality traits and powers. Practising Wicce is a process of getting in touch with and becoming attuned to spiritual energies, so we can work with them in creating magic. Knowing the Directions is part of that attunement.

Song To The Five Directions

East comes
Spreading her wings in the dawn
East comes
Singing her songs of the air
Breathing new life everywhere

South comes
Fire and passionate will
South comes
Courage, power and pride
Sparking the spirit inside

West comes
Flowing her waters and tears
West comes
Waves of the night will appear
Cleansing all sorrow and fear

North comes
Sensuous wimmin of old
North comes
Bringing the earth, rock and stone
Teaching us ways of the Crone

Spirit comes
Comes from that place out of time
Spirit comes
Opening gates to the soul
Helping to make ourselves whole

When you find the center inside of yourself
You will know the secrets of life
When you find the center inside of yourself
You will know the secrets of life

By Ffiona Morgan, with help from Artemis Lionwolf 9993

Composed for West Coast Women's Music and
Comedy Festival 1993

Direction of the East—Element of Air

Air is a symbol of the mind, thoughts, breath, and all intuitive knowledge. Her places are windswept hills, mountains, plains, high towers, and windy beaches. Air contains clouds, produces storms, whirlwinds, and hurricanes.

Invocation to the East

Goddesses and Guardians of the East,
Keepers of knowledge
Champions of justice, eyes of the mind
You of quicksilver logic and lightning thoughts
With your breath, grant us new beginnings
So we may know our truths

Great golden eagle, star-seeker, fly us on your wings
At first light of rosy pink dawn
To the watchtowers of the rising sun
Over windy beaches, cliffs and mountain peaks
Gliding and soaring on silver wings
In wide, lazy circles in the fresh spring wind
Effortlessly we fly

Breathe of life
Sacred words of power stream from my lips
In praise of Thee.
Give us knowledge and wisdom to make clear decisions
To communicate our thoughts with ease and clarity,
So we may know our truths

Breath of beginnings
Of risings of the moon, sun, bread and wimmin,
Energize us

Sharp sword of confrontation
Help us face and speak of injustice without fear
Spirit of the East, carry me home, to myself.

Wind came and knocked on
the door of my mind
I opened—and was swept away
Fresh breeze of knowing.
The Dawn of Reason.

Colors:
Gold & Red. Gold symbolizes illumination, wisdom, and enlightenment: red, vital energy. Colors of the Dawn White. The colors of the east help us to see clearly and fly high.

Astrological Signs:
Gemini, Libra, Aquarius

Gemstones:
Topaz, Rose Quartz

Animals:
All birds, especially the Eagle and Hawk

Essence of Air Energy:
Mental strength, clarity, studying,communications, decision-making, singing, peace of mind, breath, inspiration, all sounds

Powers:
To know and understand

Magical Tools:

All blades, including the athame (witch's knife), labrys and swords, bells, wings, feathers, censer, incense, musical instruments.

Goddesses of Air:

Hina - Butterfly Goddess of Polynesia
Oya - Yoruban Goddess of the wind and of wisdom
Maat - Ancient goddess of Egypt, Goddess of Justice
Sheshat - Egyptian Goddess of writing, Ruler of books and
    scribes
Themis - Greek Goddess of justice and sound counsel
Aradia - Italian witch Goddess—teaches "the
    Mother's" magic
Ix Chel -Mayan Eagle Goddess of the moon and floods
Skadi - Goddess of the North Wind, Teutonic, great
    hunter
Shing - Chinese Goddess—mother of perfect intellegence
Namagiei - Hindu Goddess of teaching and prophecy
Heh - Egyptian Goddess—revealer of wisdom
Ataentsic - Iroquois/Huron Goddess—mother of breath
    and wind
Arianhrod - Celtic Goddess of the north pole
Cardea - Goddess of the Hinge

Season: Spring   **Time:** Dawn   **Sense:** Smell

Direction of South - Element of Fire

South is the heat of summer and midday. She is energy, flame, spirit, drumbeat, heartbeat, will, blood, sap, all fires (hearth, bonfires, candles), starfire, purifications, healings, sun, heat, deserts, volcanos, eruptions and explosions. Due to the increase of the sun, her time marks the rapid growth of plants (and people).

Invocation to The South

Southern Goddesses of the warm lands
Magnolias, Hibiscus, Desert flowers
Impart the fires of your desire
Stir our hearts with your flaming will
Awaken fires within

Hail all creatures of the South
Coyote of the yellow fur
Noon Sun beating down
Bless us with your innocence and trust

Burn in us, flames of candlelight and fire
Spark of life
Riding your galloping horse
Amazon huntress of the bright heat
You streak across the hot plains
Strong will shining, victorious
We remember you

Powerful Warriors: Calafia, Cybele, Boudicea, Pele, Arrina
Defenders of wimmin, champions of the helpless
Courage and strength are your weapons against oppression
We remember you

Bright Spirited Goddess
Eyes flashing fire, burning with pride and passion
Confident in your power
Roaring red lioness in heat
The air shimmers when you walk.

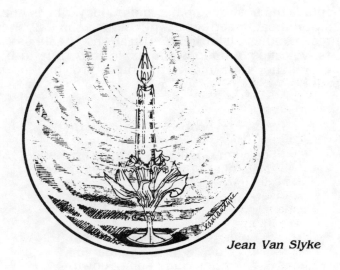

Jean Van Slyke

Then came **Fire**,
Tongues of flame
Licking at my soul
Power—Spirit—Ecstasy
Dancing in The flickering light.

Colors:
Yellow and Green (Medicine Wheel), Green is the color of
trust, healing and restoring energy, Yellow is the color of
heat, the sun, and mid-day.

Astrological Signs:
Leo, Sagittarius, Aries.

Gemstones:
Harlequin Fire Opal, Yellow Citrine Quartz.

Animals:
Lion, Coyote (Medicine Wheel),
Fire-breathing Dragon, and Horse.

Essence of Fire Energy:

Taking action, spirit, will, passion.

Powers:
To will, to take action.

Magical Tools:
Magic wand, the rattle, the drum and censor

Goddesses of Fire:
Arrina - Sun Goddess of Anatolia
Amaterasu - Sun Goddess of Japan
Brigit - Celtic Goddess of smithcraft and poetry
Calafia - Legendary revolutionary amazon of
     California
Coyotewoman - Native American Guardian of the South
Cerridwen - Goddess of the cauldron and Summer
     Solstice
Hestia and Vesta - Greek and Roman Goddesses of
     the hearth
Pele - Hawaiian Goddess of the volcanoes
Oya - Yoruban Goddess of transformation
Shakti - Hindu Goddess of supreme force, active
     aspect of eternity

Season: Summer   **Time of Day**: Noon   **Sense:** Sight

Direction of The West - Element of Water

West symbolizes emotions, intuitions and feelings, love, courage, sorrow, the ocean, tides, lakes, streams, pools, springs, wells, the womb, the unconscious mind and maturity. West is the direction of sunsets, introspection, and spiritual strength.

Invocation to The West

Streaming waters rise
Waters of Her living womb
Glory streams through our dreams
Serpent of the endless sea
Magical dolphins and sea creatures
Place of the sorrows and joys of the heart
Join us now

We hear your siren's song, the chant of the whales
We feel the pull of tides
Calling to us like a lover
Your haunting song echos through the dusk

Sunset casts her fiery, glittering rays
Illuminating the lagoon with splendor
The Evening Star twinkles in the twilight dusk
Swelling tides rise with the night
Rain that washes our bodies and souls
May we float in your arms

In the West I am older, mature, alone
Birthing myself from the watery abyss
The wellspring of myself
All the sadness of life, dreams lost
Chances missed, friends forgotten
Floods of disappointment
Tears flowing from the cup of compassion.
I take courage from the lessons of facing life alone
My robe is adorned with jewels of experience
I look inside and find myself

Guardians of darkness, be my blanket
Cover me with endless night
Birth me with the waters of your living womb
Your love streams through my heart
Cleansing me of pain.
Rainmaker, Twilight Star, ancient ocean of emotions
Tiamat, Yemaya, Aphrodite, Nammu
Hear us now, Goddesses of the water

Water...Flooding, Ebbing.
The pull of Moon on the tides of my heart.
Shifting, changing
The shores of my Self.

Colors:
Black, Indigo, Dark Blue. The blues of twilight
merge with the black of night

Astrological Signs:
Scorpio, Pisces, Cancer

Gemstones:
Black Tourmaline, Aquamarine, Lapis

Animals:
Grizzly Bear (Medicine Wheel), Water Serpents, Dolphins,
Whales, Porpoises, Sea fish, birds and mammals

Essence of Water Energy:
Feelings, emotions, maturity, intuition, unconscious mind

Powers:
To feel, to dare.

Magical Tools:
Cup or chalice, shells, all liquids, hearts,
Representations of creatures of the sea.

Goddesses of Water:

Aphrodite - Greek Goddess of passionate love

Sappho - Greek Goddess of lesbian passion/love

Mami Watu - The Mermaid, African Goddess of seduction

Yemaya - African Goddess of the ocean and the full moon

Hecate - Protector of wimmin, Goddess of the Crossroads

Kuan Yin - Chinese Goddess of peace and perfect contentment

Tiamat - Goddess of the ocean

Nammu - Sumerian Goddess of primeval ocean

Season: Autumn   **Time:** Twilight   **,Sense:** Taste

Direction of The North - Element of Earth

Earth is a symbol of the body, growth, the material plane (money), creativity, silence, nature, caves, caverns, groves, fields, rocks, standing stones, mountains, crystals, metal. It is the element of the Crone, the wise old womon.

Invocation to The North

Grandmothers and Guardians of the North
Cornerstones of all magic power
Home of the old and wise Ones
Find us a place in your stone circle

Deep in the rocky mountains, womb-like caves of your earth
In the furrows of your fertile fields
We find you waiting on frozen snowy mountains
To carry us home

Crone of the mountains, trees and forests
Grant us your wisdom
We search for you at midnight
And find that death has replaced you
Your panther coat glistening under the stars
Gleaming, your buffalo mane comforts us

Great Mothers of the Earth
Buffalo Womon, Odudua, Gaia
You who were here before us,
Who will continue after we are gone
Draw us to your abundant bosom
To partake of your prosperity
Rock us....rock us to sleep
Wrapped in your silence.

And **Earth** was there, Solid, Real.
Touched by my sensual body
Deep-yawning caverns, swollen hills
Trembling life inside The Mother
The Pregnant, Silent Earth

Colors:
Winter Earth colors—Browns, Greens, Rust, Reds, Yellows
White of the snow

Astrological Signs:
Virgo, Taurus, Capricorn

Gemstones:
Clear Quartz Crystal, Sugalite, Amazonite

Animals:
Cow or Bull, Bison, Earth Snakes,
Deer, White Buffalo

Essence of Earth Energy:
Grounding, the material world, work, money, the body
(flesh and bones) survival, rocks, creativity

Powers:
To keep silent

Magical Tools:
Pentacle, Morning Star, Crystals

Goddesses of Earth:
  Gaia - Greek Earth Mother, Goddess of our planet
  Pasowee, Buffalo Woman - Native American teacher
    and healer
  Coatlicue - Aztec Goddess of spring festivals
  Great Corn Mother - South American Goddess of the
    corn and planting
  Demeter - Greek Mother Goddess associated with
    the harvest
  Lada - Slavic Goddess of Spring
  Odudua - African Goddess of earth, planting and
    procreation
  Innana - Sumerian Goddess of love and grain
  Gauri - Hindu fertility Goddess

Season: Winter   **Time:** Midnight   **Sense:** Touch

Direction of The Center - Element of Aether

We look to the center to see what we have been searching for. The center responds, being the place of the spirit, the home of inspiration and creativity. The center of the cyclone is still and calm. While chaos rules and whirls uncontrollably, like a banshee swirling in the dance of air. The center is a haven, an oasis, a place of security, a door marked "home".

Behind the eyes, heart, brain and blood lies the center of the body, place of groundedness and a space where the soul lives, where love and hate, fear and passion are born. The center forms the words, speaks the truths, fills the gap. It is not fearful or empty. It is a place that issues forth all things of spirit. It is the aether element, where the akkashic records of all things for all time are kept.

Centers are a cup filled with tears, a vessel filled with love. We look to the center and see our lives passing through the mirrors of time, reflecting memories. The center holds the memories. Where do you go from the center? You spin outward carrying your dreams, scattering your hopes, walking in the rain, riding on the breeze.

Rejoice in your center, your space, your fifth dimension, your magic. For we are all magic and we all have our center, our place to return and be refilled, revitalized, washed clean. Believe in, and look to your center. She makes you whole.

The center extends above, below, and all places beyond the moon. The Center of the circle represents spirit, all life energy which is a manifestation of the Goddess. The Center is the void, everywhere and nowhere.

"When you cast the circle, you, yourself are the center. Within you the four elemental powers are reconciled—by the special principle, the holy center, the still point of the turning wheel, the indestructible part of you."[4]

Invocation to The Center

Hail to the Center, direction of the spirit
Goddesses of the void, place out of time
Spiralling out to hold you

The center is calm and still
Axle for the wheel of a turning, swirling world
You dive into the unknown
Like in a trance
It is hypnotic
The Goddess appears between the worlds
Keeper of the gates
She turns her key, opening them for you, opening
You enter...you take a chance

You are illuminated with the light of all colors
Music of the spheres sings her vibrant melody
You dive into the unknown world
Phoenix rising to the sky
Void out of time

You are the center
Changer and the changed.
Heart of the Goddess
Home to yourself
At last.

Judith Hower

Colors:
All colors, rainbows, purple (crown chakra color),
golden light, black light.

Astrological Signs:
Arachne the Spider, the 13th sign

Gemstones:
Spectrolite, diamond

Animals:
The Phoenix firebird who rebirths herself out of the
ashes of death and destruction, The Sphinx.

Essence of Aether Energy:
Exploration of the deeper self, transcendence,
transformation, change.

Powers:
To feel the Goddess, Still center of a whirling abyss

Magical Tools:
Cauldron, cone of power, and representations of The Goddess.

Goddesses of Aether:
Isis - Egyptian Triple Goddess
Sita - Hindu Goddess—an avatar (incarnation)
Spiderwoman - Navaho weaver of Fate
The Moirie - Greek weavers of Fate
Shekhinah - Hebrew Goddess identified with wisdom and
torches
Nephthys - Egyptian Goddess, mourner and guardian of the
dead

Time:
Place between the worlds which is a place beyond time

Season: The turning wheel   **Sense:** Hearing

Notes - Chapter 2

1. Deborah Bender, "Designing Our Own Rituals,"
   Womanspirit, , Winter Solstice 9979, Vol 6, #20.
2. Denise Brown & Dragon, "Wicce 101," *Goddess Rising,,*
   Winter Sol. 9984, p. 5.

3. First done by Jean & Ruth Mountaingrove, San Jose State,
   1974.
4. Denise Brown & Dragon, "Wicce 101,*Goddess Rising*
   Winter Sol. 9984, p. 3.

Chapter 3
Specific Rituals

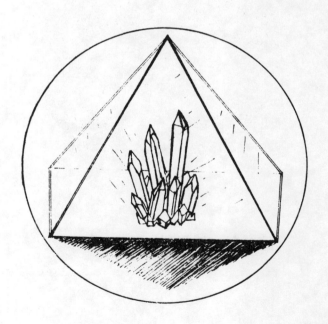

CHAPTER 3 - SPECIFIC RITUALS

**These rituals are all opened by: Smudging/Purifying,
Addressing the Directions, Invocation (Optional).
They are closed by: Thanking The Directions, Closing The Circle**

"When we do ritual, we are both enclosing ourselves in the place between the worlds and we are entering the worlds to celebrate, to heal and to make change."[1]

"When what is valued as sacred is found in this world, in the plants, animals, humans, flowers, trees and rocks, in time and in space as well as outside them, then when we look around us something that feels like love begins moving us, a sort of fierce mother love that is the Goddess inside each of us protecting her/our animal, vegetable and mineral children, wanting to set them free."[2]

RITUAL FOR RELEASING A RELATIONSHIP

This is a ritual for releasing a person, a relationship, a person to whom you must say goodbye or a situation which must end.

Write on the left-hand side of a blank sheet of paper the good things about this relationship. Write on the right-hand side of the page the difficult or negative things. Tear the paper in half. On the right side write both names (yours, and the person you wish to release). Keep the left side and set it aside. Bring your favorite magic crystal, rock, or stone, as well as a small bag of cornmeal to a special spot outdoors that you feel is "your spot".

If you live in the city, go out into nature somewhere, a private spot where you can stand on bare earth.

Crumple the right side of the paper in your hand.

Make a circle with salt nine feet in diameter (this is the traditional circumference of a magic circle). Inside this circle burn the paper you have crumpled. Scoop up the ashes and put them in a small container of some kind.

Do an offering to the five directions. Talk to the spirit of the person. Release them, but leave the door open so they might come when you call. Take a handful of cornmeal and the ashes: twirl in a circle three times. The last time let out a yell and throw the handful as far as you can.

Leave. Don't look back.

For seven days read the good things about the relationship that you have kept and set aside. At the end of this time dispose of the paper in any other way, except burning.

LETTING GO RITUAL
by Norma Joyce

Write on a piece of paper, in red ink, all the things that you want to let go of, things that you keep in your life because of Ego needs. Draw a circle and call in your helpers. Cleanse the circle with incense, and light a red candle, calling on your higher self to hear what you are asking. Light the paper from the red candle and visualize yourself as completely free of the old conditioning that is holding you back. (You need to have a dish to put the burning paper in.)

In addition to the color red being the color of the base chakra and the color we think of as pure energy, where do you think the color got that reputation? The blood that we shed each month, the blood that is shed when we are born. What could give more power? What could symbolize better, the recommitment to a new life that is totally different. A birth emerges from the red of power. Feel that color coming up into your every being, with energy and renewal of spirit. Blessed be.

FERTILITY RITUAL

This is a ritual that I designed for two of my friends who were inseminating. Plan a minimum of two hours preparation time to create sacred space and an altar. Have a paper prepared on which you have written all the reasons why you want a baby. Add the baby's proposed name to this sheet.

Light the three Maiden, Mother, and Crone candles. Wait to light the "working candle" until you actually inseminate. This candle is green, the color of fertility and the heart.

On another sheet of paper, write all your negative internalized ideas about motherhood. For example, list all messages you may have been given which say that you should not/can not be a good mother. Or, list all the things that are obstacles to your becoming pregnant. Burn this paper in a small pot on the altar and keep the ashes. Later, go to the ocean or a body of water, and throw the ashes in the water, repeating three times: "I release my spirit from these negative thoughts", followed with "As I (we) say it, so shall it be," chanted three times.

After burning the paper (above), get comfortable and prepare to inseminate. Whoever is assisting in the insemination, whether it be your partner or a friend, can massage the mother-to-be. Light the "working" green candle. Address the directions, in order:

To the East, element of Air - "With my mind and thoughts I create this child (name). Aradia, Hina, Skadi, blow your winds my way. With the power of my breath, I breathe life into her." You could also ring a bell, fan the mother with a wing, or raise your athame in the air to the east.

To the South, element of Fire - "With my will, I create this child _____, Amaterasu, Arrina, Coyotewoman, bring your passion and heat to this creation." You can shake a rattle, beat a drum, or point a wand to the south.

To the West, element of Water - "With the power of my emotions, I create this child, _____, born of water. Yemaya, Aphrodite, Hecate, Kuan Yin, bring your healing waters to speed this liquid to its destination." Water can be drunk, or scattered in the ritual space.

To the North, element of Earth - "With my body, I create this child, _____. Medicine Woman, White Buffalo Woman, Gaia, Demeter, Kore, Persephone, Lada, Great Corn Mother, All Mothers of the Earth, make my body fertile and receptive." You can hold up a small receptacle in which you have placed some earth.

To the Center, element of Spirit - "To the center, psychic element, to things we feel but cannot see. With my spirit I create this child, _____. May the Goddess bless us."

Retreive the inseminating liquid. While it is thawing, everyone can chant "Ma". Hold the container in your hands.

Chant for several minutes while the energy builds. When it is at a peak and the cone of power is formed, chant, "We release this magic energy to create our child, Blessed Be."

Ground yourself by opening up the chakras in the bottom of your feet. Pull energy up from the earth and fill your body with it. Visualize your grounding cord which attaches deep down in the earth. Inseminate. While the inseminating happens, the wimmin present can sing or chant songs appropriate to the joyous occasion. When it is done, thank the Goddesses and the five directions. Close the ritual.

BIRTHDAY RITUAL

Blowing out birthday candles is blowing out your wishes. Candles should be left burning until they are gone. If you light a candle for a spell and must put it out before it has burned, use a candle snuffer or wet your fingers.[3]

A dear woman friend came to me and asked me to create a ritual for her birthday. The following was my present.

The day was warm and sunny, and the ritual took place outside on women's land. We drew a nine foot circle in the ground with a magic wand and marked the four directions. We began by smudging with cedar, to the left, to purify and create sacred space. The Smudging was done by her friend and lover. The five directions were then addressed and we asked them to join us. We sat and passed around the Prayer Pipe that contained the herb mullein. Each woman lit the pipe and said a prayer for the birthday woman and a prayer to the earth. Next, my friend lay in the center of the circle of women (there were about 13 present)

and we chanted, in turn, all the names she had used over the course of her lifetime. This took some time. We ended with her present name and chanted until the cone of power formed in the center. As it formed she stood up and raised her arms to the heavens, while we sent the energy of the cone and chant back on her.

We then formed a birth canal with our arms and passed her, sky clad, from one end of the canal to the other, while chanting her name.

The circle was formed again and my friend walked from womon to woman, around the circle, looking deep into each one's eyes, and repeated, "You are Goddess". When she finished saying this, each woman responded to her, "You are Goddess" before she moved on to the next one.

We then gave her our gifts, which included songs and poetry. My birthday friend, who is a wonderful dancer, ended the circle by dancing for us, twirling and whirling in the twilight sunset, waving several brilliantly colored scarves. It was truly a transforming birthday.

The circle was closed. We danced and feasted for hours.....a birthday celebration we would always remember.

RENAMING RITUAL

Altar is set—Directions are addressed, circle is purified and opened.

The woman who is being named should wear something that she's never worn and purify everything she will wear during the ritual, even jewelry and glasses.. Then leave them off until after the ceremony.

This is a renaming for (insert name of the woman who is giving up her old name and taking on a new one). Going around the circle to the left, the first six women read, in turn, the following: (all writings used in the ritual should be given to participants before the ritual begins).

First Woman:
"The content of our visions can no longer be expressed in the old forms. Our visions require new concepts, new names, totally new assumptions. We need to define what our future can be and how we will work for it."

Second Woman:
"As witches, we exercise power with magic words. When others name us, we are enslaved by these names that define the ways in which we see ourselves and the world. We can transform the world and ourselves if we are the Namers, if we have found and created our own magic names that express our power."

Third Woman:

"The feminist process is one of naming ourselves; the recognition and creation of our inner and outer realities. Every woman must first remember and discover who she is, her real name, her true nature, abilities, and purpose on this planet."

Fourth Woman:

"Then she can choose to be herself, to transform into the woman she has discovered. She can discard all crippling beliefs she has held about herself, beliefs she has learned from others and from the patriarchy with all its assumptions and symbols."

Fifth Woman:

"We can heal ourselves by replacing our old, imposed beliefs with the inner knowledge that we have remembered and affirmed. We can consciously evolve, creating and naming ourselves, according to our own choices. Then we assume total, direct responsibility for who we are now."

Sixth Woman:

"Take the power in our own sweet hands,
Oh, my sisters.
Power of the sun's rise and fall,
Power in our own sweet bodies—Our wombs;
Our hands that have made bread and babies,
It lives for everyone.
Made now by us,
We build, we birth,We name ourselves."

......Author unknown

In the next part of the ritual, the woman speaks about her present name, how she got it, the herstory of it, what her life has been like living with this name, and why she wants to change it.

Another womanfriend tells the story of the new name; where it came from, its meaning, and its essence. If it is connected to a Goddess, she can tell us about this Goddess, and finally, how she sees this change affecting everyone in the circle.

The next group of women to speak follow the preceding six women in the circle and are given different pieces of paper to read. Each piece has one name that this woman has used in her lifetime, including nicknames, first and last names, married names, father's names, etc.

The seventh woman reads: "For her entire life of (her age) years, she has carried the names of men."

The eighth woman reads: "Carrying, using the names of men, gives power to them, and to their structure."

The ninth woman reads: "Names of men, patriarchal names: grandfather's names, father's names, husband's names."

The tenth woman reads: "Our power is within us. We look and listen within to find it, and our true names. In speaking our new names, we live in fidelity to our visions."

The next group of women read:

Ffiona Morgan - Dweller by the sea

Ffiona - singer, music and festival-maker, dancer

Ffiona - trusted friend, sister to women

Ffiona - potter, artist, stitcher, gardener, preparer of food, lover of the earth

Ffiona - lover, daughter, mother, and nurturer of women

Ffiona - the re-member-er, the Priestess, the Witch!

Women pass the water bowl, and each one dips her fingers into it and touches the renamed one somewhere on her body, saying the words, "I give you this name, in the name of the Goddess of ten thousand names." This is to be followed by a personal gesture of love.

The group begins a chant with "Ma" then switches to the new name. The cone of power is sent to the renamed womon to energize her new name and send healing and power to her..

The women proceed to a firepit outdoors, or a cauldron indoors, to burn the old names in the sacred fire that has been set burning. The renamed womyn puts on her new garments.

Energy is grounded and the circle is closed.

CRONE

By Ruth Barrett

Untie a knot, tie a new knot.....Bind it and set it free.
Take me in your twisted hand, old womon
With each wrinkle I am yours in the end.
Twist the twine, weaver of time
Your destiny is mine.

I raise my eyes into my eyes, and there I see you beckoning,
Conspirator, adventurer, upon the spiral way,
Whose approach is creamed away in lies
You are not refused in me,
Whose whisper now is deafening
I watch you weaving patiently.

Holy Mother of the Web, Widow of the spider's tread
Sister spinners, weavers all,
Dance upon the Harpy's claw,
Fill the void with sacred rage,
Rattle the bars and free the cage,
Shatter silence with your cries,
Sister flyers, pierce the skies!

Untie a knot..............

Like the snake that sheds its skin,
Letting transformation take me
The golden chrysalis hangs by a thread
As I look within.

Where one leaves off and the next begins,
In your chaos will I bide,
Shadow spinster, Moerae,
Guide me to the other side!

Untie a knot, Tie a new knot.....Bind it and set it free!

Available on Ruth's wonderful tape, *Parthenogenesis,*
Ladyslipper Distribution, Durham, NC, 1-800-634-6044.

CRONING CEREMONY

The Crone state of mind keeps us in touch with our endings, our aloneness (all-one-ness), and the ability of how and when to use our energy well. Crone energy is a state of mind and an aspect of every woman. A young womon can be acting from her "Crone" as well as from her "Maiden" or "Mother".

In prepatriarchal cultures, the elders (Crones) had special revered status in their communities. Wimmin of age were seen to have a unique wisdom gained from their many years of life. They looked on their age with pride, as did the members of the tribe or village. "While the Crone had ritualistic roles for many events, she had special duties and responsibilities related to death.......the Crone cared for dying persons and eased their transitions."[4]

In 1989, Renate Sky and I planned a Croning for our dear friends Rosamond and Virginia to honor their transition into the final stages of their lives. The ritual began with smudging, addressing the Directions, and opening the circle. The group of wimmin (close friends and acquaintances) sat around and listened to stories of the crones' lives. The Crones brought photos documenting specific times during the years, and these were passed around while the tales were told. Most interesting were the Crones' stories of lessons learned in their lifetimes. Because there were two women being croned, this was a long but enjoyable process.

We then took turns giving affirmations and telling stories of our experiences with the Crones. Toasts were given and libations were poured, accomplishments were spoken of, and elder Crones attending the gathering were acknowledged and praised. Flower wreaths were placed on the heads of the two Crones. They also spoke of their wishes and hopes from this group of friends, and from life in general. Plaques commemorating this special day can be made by participants and given to the Crone(s) at this time.

The group proceeded to move outside, where the Crones were presented with gifts. Some wimmin gave material gifts, some danced or sang songs, one womon gave a video of the celebration. Large amethyst crystals were given to represent the Crone Jewels.

Since I was Priestess, I presented these crystals saying, "We honor you, our Crones, with these crystals; may they always remind you that you are Goddess, our sisters, and wise wimmin. Blessed Be the Crone aspect of The Goddess—Fortress of wisdom, Cutter and Taker of life."

One womon danced a special dance, another sang a song, still another played her harp. Musicians engaged for the occasion played dance music during the ritual and afterwards for the party.

The circle was closed, directions thanked, and the feasting and merriment continued.

POLITICAL RITUALS

Ritual To Protect The Planet

The following is a ritual to protect the planet. It occurred on the 3rd of August, 1986, New York Time. It was written and coordinated by womyn in Wellington, New Zealand to correspond witn the Reclamation of the Statue of Liberty, in New York City. The invocation is as follows:

Invocation:

We, wimmin of the earth, gather in as many places as we can, acknowledging wimmin of the third world who, because of the oppression of white capitalism and patriarchy, cannot be with us.

We, lovers of earth and of each other, invoke the female powers who have existed from the beginning of time and who will outlast the particular evils of this century, whose places of power are still the stones, the leylines, the groves, the temples, the bodies, energies, and blood of wimmin, which flows with the waxing and waning of the moon and tides that harmonize with the rhythms of this planet.

We invoke the Goddesses of the old religions: Gaia, Medusa, Ceredwyn, Brigid, Sophia, Kore, Kali, Shakti, AuSet, Artemis, Ashtoreth, Ishtar, Innana, Isis, Hecate, Demeter, Nammu, Maat, Spiderwoman, Changing Woman, Asintmah, Aisehei, Fuji, Izanami, Amaterasu, Ukemochi, Freya, Iduna, Mielikki, Nana Baluku, Mama, Kwan Yin, Vari-ma-te-takere, Pele, Hina. We invoke the Great Goddess, Mother and Creator of all life. We invoke powerful wimmin of all ages, cultures, and classes, who have defied patriarchal structures and systems. We invoke the power of the thirteen million plus wimmin burned as witches during the Inquisition.

We invoke the elements of earth, fire, air, water and spirit to turn back the forces that threaten our planet and to speed up the release of wimmin energy throughout the world, so that negative, life-destroying patterns be replaced with positive, life-giving ones.

You are in the beginning before the beginning
In the end beyond the end.
Earth, Air, Water, Fire, Spirit,
Mother, Daughter, Sister, Lover, Friend
Always, wayset, womyn the way,
Forever, everfore, all-of-us eternal.

It was suggested that each group of wimmin work out their own ritual using the above, or a similar invocation, and that the ritual occur in a place of power, if possible.

> "For just as they have made the male god to rule over Our Great Mother, so they have justified their rule over you.
> Know from this that personification is political.
> And thus the yoke of your oppression is their denial of She who is the source of all life.
> Know also that as you seek to change your world I am with you.
> Have the courage then to change even what seems immutable, implacable, fixed as the stars.
> For just as the fixed stars are truly in flux, so can the unmovable be moved.
> For I am the greatest change; I am the change that changes not. I will be with you and all who return to me. For as you liberate me, so shall you be set free and the balance of the universe shall be restored."[5]

Womyn Take Liberty

On August 3, 1986, lesbians and feminists took over the Statue of Liberty, the most colossal representation of an Amazon on earth. We decided that we could not let the one and only 100th anniversary of the statue pass without making a strong, political statement for lesbians and feminists, and the causes we cherish, especially the cause of world peace. Aware that the Statue of Liberty has become the female personification of the U.S., that she has been used to sell everything from war to pornography, we envisioned us reclaiming the statue from the patriarchy and rededicating it to our values and goals.

A national network of activists committed to carrying out direct action for lesbian/feminist issues took up the idea and gave it form and substance. They spread the idea of taking/reclaiming the statue, and began planning the events of the day. Since they were an unstructured grassroots network without the resources of a centralized organization, their event was spontaneous and participatory, rather than highly choreographed and star-focused. They gathered at the statue at Liberty State Park, N. J. to stand up for lesbianism, feminism, and peace, to counter the corporate, militaristic, and nationalistic abuse of wimmin's image, and to show that we are determined to reclaim the statue and the nation for which she stands. They chose August 3rd because it marked the beginning of Hiroshima-

Nagasaki Week, Lesbian/ Wimmin's Equality Month, Lammas, and the New Moon.

The Womyn Take Liberty call says it all:

The Statue of Liberty was 100 years old in 1986. It should shock no feminist that 100 years ago womyn were excluded "for their own good" from ceremonies dedicating the statue. A century later, we gathered to demonstrate that wimmin should not be excluded from full participation in society. Wimmin loving wimmin of every race, class, and kind, sisters from across the United States and around the world gathered on Sunday, August 3, 1986 to celebrate the Statue's birthday, and to reclaim the colossal female figure which has come to symbolize our society to people all over the world. We took this action to dedicate Liberty to womyn's creativity, growth, struggles, values, and visions.

Governments and private corporations planned a ceremony for Liberty's anniversary. Although womyn were not banned from the proceedings, it was clear that the values of nationalism, militarism, male supremacy, and private enterprise, dominated their event. The original unveiling in 1886 was an orgy of military parades, speeches by generals and male politicians, fireworks, cannonades, and rifle volleys. In 1986, private corporations competed with one another to raise the money to restore an arm, chin, or nostril. They acted as though they owned her, or parts of her. It is up to womyn to keep Liberty whole, to protect her as a symbol of a whole and healthy society.

By our acts of celebration, we remind ourselves and others that the symbol of our nation is a womon. Liberty is an image of the Goddess—Athena, Lucinda, Libertas. The people of France gave her to the the people of the U.S. as an embodiment of the revolutionary values of liberty and equality. Liberty holds no swords, spears, guns, shields, nukes, or weapons of any kind. She stands in peace. The broken chains at her feet symbolize **womyn rising in resistance against all forms of domination and slavery.**

I am the door of power
Through me everything comes
And through me everything goes

Martha Courtout

DEATH RITUAL

We gather at twilight or nighttime (if possible). All bring large bunches of flowers to adorn the dead womon's coffin or ashes urn. The color white is the ancient color symbolizing death in many traditional cultures, including China and the entire Orient. Womyn attending will dress in white for the occasion. The ritual should be thoroughly read and prepared by all before it is enacted.

It is wonderful to hold this ritual outside—under an oak tree, on a beach, or by a lake. This will be determined by the wishes of the dead woman, and if no specific preference is given by her, a place can be chosen which accommodates her personality. For example, if she loved the ocean it would be fitting to have this ceremony on a private beach, if one is available. If she loved the wide open spaces, a suitable place can be found in that terrain.

All members of her coven, grove, female members of her blood, and extended family are invited. Her blood family, if not sympathetic to the woman's pagan worship, might have another service for her, and her grove or coven will not have access to her ashes or body. Then, a creative mixing of earth, salt, sand, and clay can be used to symbolize her body remains for the ritual.

All gather. The ashes or casket is placed in the center of the circle. Flowers are laid around the urn or casket. The Altar is ringed with 13 white candles (symbolizing death). If it is outside and windy, the candles can be placed in glass containers. The circle is cast and the directions addressed. The candles are lit, clockwise to the left, by the persons closest to the dead sister. All wimmin hold hands.

Priestess:

"We have gathered in our sacred circle to honor our beloved sister witch Elizabeth, and to send her to her resting place between incarnations. We invoke Kali, She who destroys, then awakens us to new life; Hecate, She who stands at the crossroads of life and death; Cerridwen, The White Sow, who carries us home; Spiderwomon Life Weaver; and Goddess of Fate, Mari, She who guides the dead on their path by the rays of her body, the moon.

"Hail, Death, Powerful Crone of the Universe." The Priestess holds up a cup of red drink (fruit juice or wine) to the sky and chants, "To Death." Circle members chant "To The Goddess." As this happens, the cup is passed. Each womon takes a sip. When the cup returns to the Priestess, she pours a libation on the earth.

The wimmin now speak positive affirmations, to the left, clockwise, each repeating **short** phrases, such as "She made me laugh", "She cared for me when I was sick," "She was a great teacher to me"—any and all expressions of love and remembrance.

The following song is chanted:

> "Listen, listen, listen to my heart's song,
> Listen, listen, listen to my heart's song.
> I will never forget you, I will never forsake you,
> I will never forget you, I will never forsake you.
> "Listen, listen, listen to my heart's song, (repeat)
> I will always remember, I will always be near you (repeat)

Priestess:
"We picture you now, Elizabeth, smiling, happy, your spirit in ecstasy, free from the bounds of the earth plane."

The white candles are extinguished with a snuffer (don't blow them out), again moving clockwise, and the circle stands in the night.

Priestess:
"We shall not fear the darkness, remembering it leads to wisdom. We shall not fear death, remembering it leads to rebirth. We shall not fear the unknown, remembering that The Goddess is at the heart of it."[6]

All candles are relit, one by one, by different wimmin. A chant begins while they are lit:

> **Blessed be, Blessed be**
> **the transformation of energy.**
> ....repeat and repeat....
> and another chant begins:

> Listen, listen, listen to my heart's song (repeat)
> I will never forget you, I will never forsake you (repeat)
> Listen, listen, listen to my heart's song (repeat)
> I will always remember, I will never forget you

Priestess:
"We offer your body to the Earth Mother, Goddess who birthed us all, and to who we all return. Blessed be!"

The body is then buried in the earth or the ashes are distributed; a few particles of the ashes of the dead womon are then sprinkled on the earth near a tree, or into the wind, into the water or lake.

Priestess:
"I hear the voices of the Banshees crying." The Banshees are Irish Goddesses who wail and cry when someone is dying.

The group begins to make mourning cries; the wails and the moans of grief. Chanting is begun until it reaches a peak. When the energy is right, the Priestess sends the cone of power to the spirit of the dead sister to help in her transformation into the land of Caer Arianrhod.

Arianrhod (Goddess of the Silver Wheel) is a Welsh Goddess of death and rebirth. Her home is Caer Arianrhod, the place where souls go to rest between incarnations; first to the crown of the North wind, and then to the disk of stars that never sink below the horizon near the Pole star. The ritual path to this sacred place is a spiral, going counterclockwise in, and clockwise out.[7]

Priestess:

"Hail Arianrhod, Goddess of Death and Rebirth, Lady of the Silver Wheel of stars. Send our sister on the sacred path to the crown of the North Wind, and then home to Caer Arianrhod, that disk of stars around the pole—that never set, that remain there as a resting place for the Ones who Wait. Oh, Great Goddess Hecate, Kalma, Mari, Belili, Gela, Sina, we release the spirit of our beloved Elizabeth to your arms. Chemnu, Mehen, Menkheret, Anumati, and Hecate, guide her to the Holy Place of Waiting. Blessed be!"

Group: "Blessed be."

Circle is closed, directions thanked, Feasting/celebrating begin.

DARK MOON SCRYING RITUAL
by Norma Joyce and Ffiona Morgan

Circle is saged/cedared and is opened. Directions are addressed.

The wimmin form the circle, chant, raise the cone and repeat:

> **"The light of our Sister Moon is hidden tonight**
> **Bring now the water that comes from Her tides**
> **Bring now the power of The Crone and the dark**
> **To guide, love, and bless us."**

A bowl of water is then brought to the circle and placed in the center. A copper bowl gives off special vibrations for scrying, but a white china bowl is also good. The womyn repeat:

> **"The light of our Mother Moon is hidden tonight,**
> **Bring us the light that She kindles**
> **Show now the power of The Crone and the dark**
> **To guide, love, and protect us."**

The candles are lit and placed in each womyn's personal holder in front of her, around the copper bowl of water. The womyn repeat:

> **"The light of our Crone Moon is hidden tonight**
> **Bring forth the life she creates**
> **Show now the power of the Hag and the dark**
> **To love, guide, and bless us."**

Incense (sage, cedar, or whatever you choose for the Dark Moon) is lit and flowers are brought into the circle. The wimmin repeat:

> **"The soma (life energy) is high, new energy waits**
> **In the arms of the New Moon, Maiden Diana**
> **We feel your waxing about to be**
> **We feel Her growth, now pray us See."**

The women look into the water, with soft eyes, and open to the images the Goddess sends. After a time the Priestess chants: **"Now let us feel the energy."**

All womyn put their fingers in the bowl and touch the water to their foreheads and temples (thumbs on temples). A new "Ma" chant is started, and continued until it peaks. The energy is sent to the scrying. After a time, they repeat:

> **"I go forth bearing soma so sweet**
> **I go forth with new energy and blessings**
>
> **I am loved, cared for, protected**
> **So mote it be."**

The Priestess grounds the energy and closes the circle.

RITUAL FOR SURVIVORS
OF INCEST, RAPE AND BATTERING

Ffiona Morgan is available to travel and perform this ritual with groups of womyn in need of healing She can be contacted at the address and phone number on the "Contributors" page at the beginning of this book.

Enter circle with the ritual, "From women you are born into this circle"(p.33). Ritual is opened by smudging and purifying with salt water.

The directions are invoked, the circle is cast. White candles (for death and purification) are placed on the altar and lit, to the left, by several women. All women wear white or silver outer garments of mourning. Under them are worn costumes of bright colors. Those womyn who fear attack or repercussions from doing this magical work may want to wear something silver to reflect back with lunar light any animosity that is felt. The Priestess of this circle should be a survivor. It is suggested the ritual be done at the Dark Moon when her Crone aspect is most powerful.

Part I. The Mourning

Priestess:

"We are in mourning for our innocent childselves. We grieve for the naivete and joy of those tender spirits, the fresh green sprouts of our youthful ones. We work this rite to connect with this part of ourselves who has lost the ability to speak."

All Womyn:

Chant in mourning tones, wailings, loud mournful cries, tears, howling to the Goddess until everyone has expended her grief. The circle keeps wailing low as different women chant the following invocations. This should take about 15-20 minutes.

First Womon:

"We invoke Hecate, Goddess of Death and Rebirth, Avenger of Womyn, Guardian of the Crossroads of Time, and Dweller in the Underground Caves. O Crone of the darkness that contains not only the underground caverns of our psyches and the memories of our abuse, but the warm moist seeds for planting our futures. Avenge our enemies and protect us from further harm at their hands. We stand at your sacred crossroads, the place of our transformation, and choose the road to life. May we walk in beauty and joy."

Second Womon:

"We call upon Kali Durga, Destroyer and Awakener. O, Kali, help us destroy the pain of those memories that keep us in sorrow, and awaken to the intense joy of life in the present, realizing the present is all we have, for it contains the past and the future."

A small bowl or basket containing small black tourmaline crystals for protection and safety, is passed clockwise around the circle and each womon takes one.

Third Womon:

"These are stones of protection which deflect negative energy and absorb internal negativity by carrying it out of our body and grounding it in the body of Mother Earth. With these magic stones we create a shield, which gives us the space to become more positive...Wear them well!"

Part II. The Healing

Priestess:

"We invoke Kuan Yin, the Healer, most Compassionate One, She who we call upon in our hour of greatest need. We call on

Buffalo Womon, Healer of the Body and Teacher of the Sacred Womyn's Ways."

Fourth Womon:

(If the circle is small, these parts can be repeated by the same womon)

"We are here now to heal our psyches and bodies of abuse. We have howled our pain to the wind and each other. May we now place strong and powerful images of healing in our hearts and spirits, to affirm our lives as positive and work for our complete and total recovery.'

Fifth Womon:

"Our memories are our past. Let us now create a place for unwanted memories that keep us from growing, feeling, and fully appreciating the love and beauty of life, the incredible dimension of our opportunities. Now create this place...take all unwanted memories of your abuse and place them there. Seal this cave, this watery abyss, this fire which burns to ashes, this howling wind that carries the memories far, far away. Lay them to rest. Tell them to leave us in peace." Participants chant:

> "Seal the cave...leave us in peace
> Seal the cave...let us be
> Seal the cave...leave us to love
> Blessed Be...Blessed Be...Blessed Be."

As this is chanted, all wimmin remove outer white clothes of death. The white death candles are blown out, and brilliantly-colored ones lit, one for each chakra. This is all done clockwise.

Part III. The Commitment
by Ffiona Morgan and Rainbow

Beginning with The Priestess, and moving to the left, each womon repeats **The Pledge,** the words of power.

I, Ffiona, am a survivor of the patriarchal wars. I recognize myself as an Amazon, blessed by the Goddess with incredible strength and crystal clarity. Having survived the attempted murder of my spirit, I pledge my support and empathy to all sisters everywhere who have likewise survived—and to those who did not. I further pledge to my body and spirit all the nurturing she needs to heal. She shall have love and acceptance from my conscious self; patience, healthy habits, abundant joy and delight, and a deep and secure faith in her healing. I will love myself.

(If a womon feels she cannot memorize all of this pledge, she can write it out on a small card and bring it with her. All should be encouraged to memorize it, so it can be repeated as an affirmation in the days to come.)

Everyone joins hands and raises them above their heads, repeating "I will love myself," and "As we say it, so will it become," repeated three times.

Now the Cone of Power is raised by chanting "Ma" or Goddess names. When the energy is raised, The Priestess will send it back to shower on the wimmin of the circle, envisioning rainbow light from the cone washing us clean and filling us with love.

Circle is closed.

Overcoming Poverty/Creating Prosperity

When you first walk in your home, look to the left-hand
corner and observe what appears there. This is the
prosperity corner of your house. The right-hand
corner is the relationship corner. You might want to
change the items that appear in these corners.

The following is excerpted from Catherine Ponder's
Open Your Mind to Prosperity, and adapted by Ffiona
Morgan to fit the needs of feminists.

Many of us with poverty, hippy, or working–class backgrounds, or those of us who adopted radical ideas during the blossoming of socialism and feminism in the late 60's and 70's, have the belief-system that it is bad to have money and desirable to be poor and struggling. For many years poverty was "groovy" and desirable, and those who aspired to upward mobility were shunned as politically incorrect. We learned that downward mobility was what we should emulate, and that if we do have money we must have stolen it or oppressed someone to get it. We believe we deserve to be poor because our families were.

Those who adopted downward mobility purely as a political stance have now abandoned those ideas and returned to middle-class values, following in the paths of their parents. Those of us who grew up poor or leftist, and those wimmin (whatever class) who still truly believe in those political ideas, are now left with the accompanying poverty-consciousness which still operates in our subconscious, keeping us from the abundance we deserve.

Abundance and prosperity are natural states of being. The Goddess wants us to be abundant because it is Her divine plan. In doing rituals for prosperity, we come to believe that we are not petitioning for help She does not want to give, but that we have the right to be abundant and the Goddess wants us to be. In fact, our spiritual growth is complemented by our abundant state of mind. Knowing, and truly believing this allows our creativity to blossom. Remember, Goddess is our source and we, as womyn, are also our own source because the Goddess is within us. The world and things of the world are not our source. In order to achieve abundance it is first necessary to rid ourselves of the belief system that prosperity is evil. The following are steps to follow in creating this consciousness and the resulting abundance.

Use one red working candle for survival and money to signify the first chakra and one green working candle to signify the heart chakra.

Step 1
Cutting Unwanted Energies and Creating a Vacuum

Invoke the Crone image as the Cutter, cutting away that which is no longer needed. Invoke Earth Crone for the material plane, Water Crone for relationships and feelings, Fire Crone for taking action, and Air Crone, (especially the Goddess Ix Chel) for dispelling limiting ideas. Calling on Kali, She who breaks down structures, is also very powerful. (Structures are represented by Kali, The Tower, in the tarot.) Visualize her lightning bolts shattering your structures.

"Cutting" creates a vacuum, or space, for prosperity. This means house cleaning; throwing out things you no longer want and establishing an order to your life. It also means letting go of any relationships or conditions that are no longer useful for your growth. Ideas which you took on, not because you passionately believed in them or that they have proven to be true for you, but because they seemed convenient and plausible at the time, can now be eliminated from your outdated belief system. Repetitive actions done purely out of habit should now be considered and unworkable ones rejected. Weeding of your personal belongings and giving away unwanted items to friends keeps the material plane circulating and avoids congestion. One of the laws of the universe is to give. If you don't give, it will be taken from you. Make a list of whatever you want eliminated from your life.

Step 2
Manifest List

Prepare a "Manifest" list of things you wish to attract. Prepare several affirmations to help you achieve the prosperity you seek, such as the ones listed below. Draw a picture of the prosperity you wish to create. This can also be done by using cut-out pictures from magazines and photos to form a collage.

After you have written the "Manifest" list and created your affirmations, color the picture you have drawn. Whether you use a collage or draw and color your picture, make sure you keep it uncluttered. Keep your artwork private; don't show or tell anyone. Carry this picture around with you and look at it often—especially before you sleep.

Make a list of what you have now that you are thankful for and give thanks as a part of your prosperity rituals.

Ideas to help you create your prosperity ritual: Be as creative as possible. Speak affirmations such as:

"I am a prosperous and abundant woman."
"I have enough money for my uses, and always will."
"I have many friends and much love."
"I am a healthy, robust woman in touch with my body."
"In the name of Habondia, Lakshmir, and Gaia—Goddesses of Plenty"

Don't focus on the past and what you didn't have, or have lost. It's better to visualize yourself in the present and the future, as abundant and happy. This way you give energy to the positive, rather than the negative. Giving energy to positive feelings or ideas gives them power and paves the way for manifesting.

Step 3
Spirit Help

Ask the Goddess for help. She wants you to be prosperous. Trust in Her, release your life to Her, and let Her guide you. Believe in Her love and the love of the universe. Call your perfect life plan into being: that of health, happiness, and abundance.

Step 4
Forgiveness

Practice forgiveness and compassion for those you hate or resent. This is a difficult step to accomplish, but believe you can do it. Ask for help. Repeating the following affirmation is helpful.

"I forgive anyone who has offended me, I release them."
"I forgive all women who have hurt me."
"I ask all women who I have hurt to forgive me."
"I am free and I free others."
"All things are clear between us, now and forever."
"Everyone I have offended now forgives me—The Goddess in thems forgives and frees me."

Step 5
Letting Go

Release to the Goddess those you love, as well as all troublesome situations or anything else you want to release. The following affirmation can be useful. Put the *Reversal* tarot card (traditionally called *Hanging One, The Hanged Man*) on your altar and meditate on it. It symbolizes letting go. Repeat the following affirmation.

"Goddess frees me from all attachments to people, places and things. Everyone and everything who is not part of my perfect life plan now releases me."

MONEY RITUAL
Using the Chakra System of Candle Burning

Have three candles on your altar: one to symbolize the Maiden, one for The Mother, and another for The Crone aspect. I use cream or a pale pastel color candle to represent the Maiden; red, maroon, deep rich green, orange, or any rich, vibrant color for the Mother; and a purple, maroon or indigo candle for the Crone. In addition, I have one "working" candle (in this case a red one), to represent the first chakra, or survival, as money is a survival issue.

Bring your symbols of affluence and all your money, cash, credit cards, or books recording your money transactions, bank statements, etc., and place them on the altar in front of your red working candle. Purify your ritual space with cedar and sage. Call to the five directions for help.

Carve your personal symbol of abundance on the red candle, and then light it. As you do, ask the Goddess Habondia to help you obtain exactly what you need for your purposes—no more and no less. Repeat out loud:

"If She Wills It—So Shall It Be."

Bless your pile of money and symbols of money, and out of the pile draw a bill. It can be as much as you feel is just: $1, $5, $10, $20, etc. Burn this bill using your red candle to light it. Repeat:

Send this money back to me,
Many times, I ask of thee
May it give me peace from want
And I will pass it on...

At this point, insert anything that you wish into the ritual. Burn the red candle all the way down. This can take hours, so you may wish to depart from your altar while it burns. Please protect your environment from fire and do not leave the house. Thank the Goddesses and directions for their help. Close your ritual.

Abundance Affirmation

I am one with the infinite riches of my subconscious mind.
It is my right to be abundant, happy and successful.
Money flows to me freely, copiously, and endlessly.
I am forever conscious of my true worth.
I give of my talents freely
I am wonderfully blessed with financial abundance.

THE DAILY RITUAL OF TAI CHI
by Janet Seaforth

Some practice Tai Chi at sunset or in the middle of the day, but I rise with the sun, put on my sweats, and go outside to greet the day with my tai chi ritual. I walk the well-worn path to my meditation spot, a fairly flat grassy area in the meadow next to the woods, find my center, and bow to the north—direction of the unknown—paying respects to another new day about to unfold. Tai Chi begins. The slow movements are based on the natural movements of animals and forms of nature. Peaceful energy flows through my body, waking my every cell, warming, nourishing, refreshing and rejuvenating me with healing energy as the slow breaths enter my body.

By Sue Sellars, 1990

The fresh air fills my entire being, from head to toes. The slowly learned movements are natural to me now. The calm easy greeting of the eight directions (in Tai Chi we address the four directions, plus the corners). Earth, Air, Water, Fire - Mountain, Lake, Thunder, Wind. I move with grace, finding my balance, acknowledging the subtle differences each day offers. There is also comfort   in knowing that millions of other people, especially in China, are also doing Tai Chi at the same time.

Today I am recovering from a cold but I still move with complete relaxation, consciously willing the healing life-breath energy into my body, filling my lungs, as I feel strength returning. I find myself in deep meditation as I do the familiar movements: 'Wave Hands Like Clouds', 'Return To The Mountain', The Golden Phoenix Rises'. I remember to move slowly, taking time to heal. 'White Crane Stands On One Leg', 'Fair Woman Works The Shuttle'--the 108 movements come to an end.   I set aside Sunday morning to practice Tai Chi with my sisters. We meet in the quiet park at 9 a.m. and do our warm-up circles and stretches together until everyone is present. Sometimes we are silent, sometimes we share a story or announce an event, or bring up an ethical question. Or maybe we agree to consult the *I Ching Book of Changes,*, one of the texts used in the understanding and practice of Tai Chi.

The form begins again as we face the north. The peaceful energy is the same as in solitary practice, but it has expanded. Tai Chi begins; the movements in harmony, integrating each woman's spirit, mind, and body. We all move as one -- sisters united, together in the silence. 'Pressing Heaven, Pressing Earth', 'Sweep the Lotus', 'Reach for the North Star', 'Ride the Tiger', 'Clouds Touch the Mountaintops'. The slowness puts us into a semi–trance as it alters our consciousness, clearing a space for the mind to have new perspectives, for the body to unblock it's tight places, and for the spirit to soar with visions of peace and the harmony of at–one–ment. The movements end. We stand together in the stillness, hear the birds sing, feel the breeze on our faces, the good earth under our feet, uniting us, as we are washed with bliss and peaceful energy.

We slowly come back to the events of the day, turn and bow to each other, in respect to the community and our individual differences.

In the spring we bring our staves, long poles of rattan, bamboo, or hardwood. We practice a fighting form, we learn the use of weapons, the vulnerable areas of our opponents, using our strength against their weakness. We commit to taking care of ourselves. The forms become more martial at times — 'Reach out and Block', 'Strike with Beak', 'Withdraw Sword', 'Elbow Strike', 'Cobra Strike' and the 'Pa Qua Kicks'. The movements comfort me: I know I can defend myself. I am confident, skilled, and thankful for the freedom and the mobility that the self defense aspect of Tai Chi has given me.

I take my staff home and carefully place it by the door so I can take it with me in the morning. The morning is my special time of nurturing myself with Tai Chi – the 20 minutes a day that gives me all the time in the world. I am learning the strange lesson that if you slow down you get there sooner. I cherish this time when I nurture and provide for myself with this daily discipline.

judith hower ©1990

TAI CHI

Today I danced with bliss
Two minutes passed
Count down the bones of life
Deep breaths they calm my soul

In peace with land at last
Last rays of day
Splash down my quiet hills
I hear the ocean's roar

Tai Chi, tai chi
My blessings come
On floating clouds of angel hair
A tiger, snake, and monkey too
Play on my body's shores again
With you.

Wrapped in your stork and crane I sleep
Protected from the maddening world
Soft wings enfold my tender soul
And give me love that I can keep.

Ffiona Morgan

TRYSTING, WEBBING, OR BONDING CEREMONY
I am writing this from the viewpoint of two
womyn, but the ceremony can be
used for any two people

When performing a Trysting, or a 'Webbing' bonding ceremony the physical place should be smudged before you begin and Sacred Space created. A beautiful altar with a profusion of flowers can be set.

Lovely music, chosen by the two wimmin can be playing while they enter and proceed to the altar.

A young maiden or child enters with a bouquet of roses and hands each participant a rose.

The Priestesses (one will do, but two is best) smudge the two people as they approach the altar, and sing:

Love, love, love, love
Wimmin we are made for love
Love each other as ourselves
For we are love.

The Priestesses address the five directions, as in opening a circle. They take turns speaking the following words to the elements.

Priestess:

'Great Isis, bringer of new life, and Sappho, Goddess of poetry and lover's inspiration, we invite your airy blessings. May the love of these two,_____ and _____, take wings and fly. Blessed Be.

Priestess:

Amaterasu, Goddess of passion and power, we invite your presence into this tryst. Pele, Goddess of excitement and joy, may your passion live forever in the hearts. of the two womyn who stand before you now. Blessed Be.,

Priestess:

Aphrodite, force of passionate love, Goddess of ecstasy and creative inspiration, power that moves the universe and awakens desire, be with _____and _____ as they share their vows to each other. Blessed Be.

Priestess:

Astarte, Demeter, Earth Mothers of love and fertility, Flora, Goddess of Beauty, bring your material abundance, your health and love of our earth to this bonding. Blessed Be.

Priestess:
Sita, Spiderwoman, Shekhinah, Goddesses of the Center,
Home of Spirit, fly your phoenix firebird to transform these
lives. May____ and ____ always feel the Goddess in their lives.
Blessed Be.

The two women will then talk about how they met and discuss
the representations of The Goddess they have brought to the
altar and what they mean to each of them. They will then tie a
candle with ribbon to signify their joining together. The
Priestesses chant very softly while this is being done:

O Aphrodite, Golden and divine
Mine the embrace and mine the kiss
The five-pointed star of love and bliss
Here I greet you, love of mine.

If more time is needed, Priestesses will sing, 'Crone' from
Ruth Barret's tape (See the bottom of page 66 for information on
how to order).

Now is the time for gifts. The women gift each other and
explain the special significance of their gifts.

Jumping the broom:

The broom symbolizes fertility, May your union
be fertile in love, passion, communication,
abundance and health .

The two womyn jump the broom. Trumpet music comes on
(optional). Everyone sings 'Love, Love (see above)' or another
song.

A special reading of a favorite story or poem, perhaps by
Sappho, is now done by the Priestess, It should be selected by
the womyn being trysted and have some special meaning to them.

Now is the time for promises. The Priestess addresses them:

In equality and mutual respect for any possible changes
or differences, please read your vows.

The vows, written by each woman, and brought to the
ceremony, or memorized and recited, will be given now.
The rings are then taken off the altar, and the Priestess asks:

**Do you vow with this ring that you will stay
together as long as it is positive for you both?
Do you promise to love each other always, lovers or not?**

The women answer. If they wish to change their names, they should state so at this time.

Libations: Cider or wine is poured into the chalice and the women cross arms and feed each other, repeating, "May you never thirst".

They then feed cherries to each other and say, "May you never hunger". After this they move around the circle and feed cherries to all present..

This is the end of the ceremony and time to close the directions.

Priestess: "We have honored the energy of the elements within us. We are Goddess, we are transformers, we are change.

Other Priestess: "We are earth, we are substantial, we are wise and we are old, We are grounded. Thank you earth. Blessed Be."

Priestess: "We are water, we are clear, we are fluid, we are vital, we are renewed. Thanks to water."

Other Priestess: "We are fire, we are bright, we are hot, we are intense, we are passionate, we are aroused. Thank you fire."

Priestess: "We are air, we are light, we are movement, we are open, we are changed. Blessed Be to air."

All Sing "May the circle be open" (See closing rituals, page 38)

Artemis Lionwolf assisted Ffiona Morgan in writing and performing this ritual, May, 9993.

BINDING RITUAL FOR SELF DEFENSXE

This is a ritual for the purpose of "binding" someone's energy who is trying to commit violence against you or another innocent person. Some witches object to bindings. One thing is certain, it's advanced magic and should not be used by beginners. I see bindings as a ritual to be used only in extremely dangerous times, where someone is actually out to do you physical harm, and you know it as fact. Sending energy back to its source is not an act of violence but a right, and we have the right to protect ourselves.

Jean Van Slyke

In using bindings for self-defense, we do not create violent behavior. Wimmin should be able to use any form of self-defense, rather than be helpless victims of womonhaters and misogynists. One method of sending energy back to its source is to visualize mirrors surrounding you so that none of this negative energy can get through. You can also surround yourself with a circle of labrys for protection. I include the following ritual for those who wish to use it and who have the skills.

SPELL TO BIND A RAPIST, BATTERER, OR KILLER OF WOMYN

> This ritual was written for an African American
> woman who was being attacked.
> Please adapt the wording for your own use.

by Linnea Almgren

Send Him A Nightmare

A nightmare is a visit from a very powerful woman. Often she sits on the chest of her victim, causing a feeling of suffocation and oppression. She also brings anxiety attacks in dreams. She will leave when she pleases.

Cast the Circle, Call the Spirits

Powers of the East, First Inspiration
Powers of the South, Anger's Sharp Edge
Powers of the West, Rushing Waters
Shape of the Thing, The Plan
Powers of North, The Earth,
Touch of the Thing—As it Is

Invoke The Darkness

Shadows, Contrasts, Behind, Under, Other
Night Sky—before and after light
Dark Earth beneath roots
Holding, Feeding, Permitting Life, Time, Change

Binding Spell

Dark womon on a dark horse
Ride three times around the man
Swirl your soft cloak around him
Show him the silence, the emptiness
He falls into, forever falling
Let the shadow of every living thing
Remind him of the emptiness within
Turn his eyes inward to see the horror of harmful acts
Hold him from harming any living thing
Bind all negative energies, within and without

Freedom Spell

Dark womon on a dark horse
Ride three times around us
Lend us protection to walk unseen
Past danger, seen but unseen

Thank you for choice, To pick it up, or set it down
Thank you for freedom to come and go, like the wind

If it be best for the universe......So Be It

A Chant Against Enemies

I stand in magic circles of spiralling energy
That nothing may cross.

Notes - Chapter 3

1. Lauren, _Reclaiming,_ Spring 1982, Vol. 1, No. 5.
2. Norma Joyce, _On Wings,_ Vol. V, Nos. I and II, 1987.
3. This idea put forth by Z. Budapest in _Grandmother of Time,_ (
    NY: Harper & Row, 1989).
4. Jacquelyn Gentry and Faye Seifert, "Crone Celebration", _Of A
    Like Mind_, Autumn 9989.
5. Judith Laura, _She Lives!_, (Freedom, CA: Crossing Press 1989)
    p. 24.
6. Janet and Stewart Farrar, _The Witches' Goddess_, (WA: Phoenix
    Pub.Inc., 1987).
7. Ibid.

Chapter 4
Sacred Wheel of the Year

While writing this chapter I realized that the structure and system of *The Wheel* pays an inordinate amount of attention to celebration of the light, and very little to celebration of the dark. In order to create a non-racist womanspirit, this must be changed. If Summer Solstice (longest day) was a celebration of the Light, then Winter Solstice (longest night) must have been a celebration of the Dark to our ancient foremothers, and should be celebrated as such. The lack of attention to the dark is "whitewashing" in the broadest sense and is inherent in the structure of Wicce itself. Therefore, feminist Wicce, which is a facet of traditional Wicce, should also be examined for racism. I welcome suggestions. . . . .   Ffiona Morgan 9994

CHAPTER 4   SACRED WHEEL OF THE YEAR

The stories accompanying the various holyday rituals do not necessarily reflect the qualities of that point on the wheel, although effort has been made to correlate the two.

In the Pagan traditions of Europe there are eight Holy Days which are celebrated to honor the changing of the seasons and the cycles of growing things. Just as there are sacred places on our earth which are imbued with magic, there are also sacred points in time when we are able to experience this same magical energy. We call these holydays "Sabbats" "The window of power opens at these profoundly significant times."[1] A womon who celebrates these holydays is called a Witch.

The ancient festivals celebrate and revere the cycles of life: birth, maturity, death, and always—change. They are deep, ancient, lunar-based, sacred and mysterious points in time. As are all rituals, they are a form or medium through which we may transcend our mundane reality, and move between the worlds to Sacred Goddess Space, a place out of time. It is thought that on these days there appears an opening in the crack between the worlds. Holydays are celebrated at the two **Solstices**, and **Equinoxes** (the **Quarter Holidays**), and on the **Cross-Quarter Holidays** of **Brigit, Beltane, Lammas** and **Samhain.** They are a recognition of the changes in the cosmos and a personal celebration of our cycles as women.

"The seasons have a rhythm, a natural energy that peaks and declines, like the waves of the ocean. They are the indicators of the ebb and flow of nature. The Cross-Quarter holydays, which occur in the fixed signs of Taurus, Leo, Scorpio and Aquarius are called the Power Gates. They release the beginning of an elemental power tide that recharges our magical batteries, drawing down the power current (magic) from the opening between the worlds.'[2]   It's easier to work with the tides when you know when they occur.

As we celebrate each Sabbat we remember the same one we celebrated the previous year, and the year before that, and the meaning of the holyday builds on all our past experiences. As we mark the seasons with our own personal changes, celebration of these times becomes a psychological metaphor for those changes.

SACRED WHEEL OF LIFE

Guardians of the Wheel of Life/Wheel of the Year are Spiderwoman, Life Weaver of the Hopis, and Cardea, Roman Goddess of the Hinge who presided over the four cardinal winds. Srinmo, Crone Goddess of Tibet, holds the cosmic wheel and Dike, the winged Goddess of Greece, turns it.

The Solstices mark the boundaries of light and darkness. **Winter Solstice** is the day when there is **less light** on the planet, the Northern point on the wheel, when the nights are longest. It is our most inward and reflective time. From that point until Summer Solstice, the light increases. **Summer Solstice** is the time of **maximum light**, the Southern point on the wheel, when the days are longest. It is also the most outward, active period of the entire year, when the light again begins to wane until Winter Solstice..

Spring and Fall Equinox are the midpoints in energy between the solstices and mark **equal day and night.**

Breaking it down even further, the midpoints between the Solstices and Equinoxes are the **cross-quarter holydays** of Brigit (Candlemas), Beltane, Lammas and Samhain (Hallomas).

Each season of the wheel begins with a **cardinal sign** at the **Solstices and Equinoxes. Cardinal** energy is energy radiating outward, the initial outpouring of each element. Cardinal energy initiates and generates activity.

Capricorn, cardinal earth sign, begins at Winter Solstice, December 21st (some years the date is off from the 21st).

Aries, cardinal fire sign, begins at Spring Equinox, March 21.

Cancer, cardinal water sign, begins at Summer Solstice, June 21st.

Libra, cardinal air sign, begins at Fall Equinox, September 21st.

Each season reachs her peak in a **Fixed** sign on the **cross-quarter holydays** of Brigit, Beltane, Lammas and Samhain, It is a time for sustaining, organizing and maintaining, giving us the power to "carry on".

Winter peaks in the fixed air sign of Aquarius, at Brigit, February 2nd.

SACRED WHEEL OF LIFE

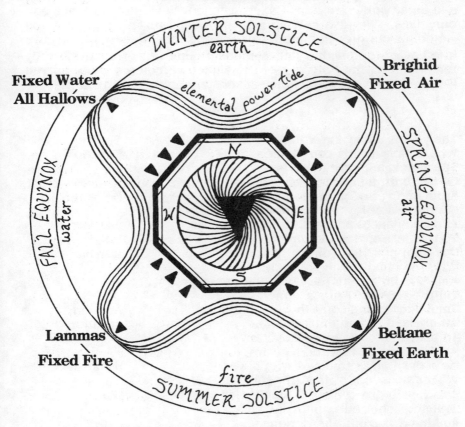

Spring peaks in the fixed earth sign of Taurus at Beltane, on May 1st.

Summer peaks in the fixed fire sign of Leo at Lammas, on August 1st.

Fall peaks in the fixed water sign of Scorpio at Samhain, on October 31st.

The **Mutable** elements, or signs, occur at the **end of each season** to culminate, transform, change and dissolve the energy in preparation for the coming season of birth and beginnings (the cardinal signs). The mutable signs are Gemini, Virgo, Sagittarius, and Pisces.

The names of the ancient festivals of Brigit and Samhain (pronounced "Sow-win") were changed by the Catholic Church, to Candlemas (Mass of the candles) and Hallomas (Mass of the Dead). For this reason I use the older traditional Celtic names, when possible, to reclaim them as our own.

We create our sabbat rituals to be a link between the outer and inner worlds, to bring us into wholeness with the cosmos and ourselves. We also celebrate to connect with each other when we honor our growth and changes of the recent season. "We live in a linear world with a linear mindset gone out of control."[3]   By remembering the holydays of the wheel we celebrate our sacred womon cycles, as well as the seasons and cycles of the earth.

Seasonal Magic

The year is a dancing womon	Spring
Who is born at the coming of spring	Equinox
The year is a dancing womon	
Of Her birth and Her death we sing...	
From spring She grows to power	Beltane
'Til the red of Her moonbloods come	
And She dances and spins toward Summer	Summer
To the beat of Her passion's drum	Solstice
'Tis then that Her womb's made fertile	Lammas
With the child that is to come	
And She flows with the Love that feeds us	
Till the Harvest Time is done	
Then dances and spins towards Darkness	Autumn
All dressed in autumn's fires	Equinox
To descend to the time of shadow	
And rest from the world's desires	
Now Her hair is touched with silver	Samhain
Winter's wisdom claims Her soul	
And She births the spirit within Her	Winter
Bringing light and hope to us all	Solstice
Igniting a blaze in the darkness	Brigit
To kindle the coming spring	
Then dreams 'til her resurrection	Spring
And Her story again begins.....	Equinox
The year is a dancing womon	
Who is born at the coming of spring	
The year is a dancing womon	
Of Her birth and death we sing	

By Shekhinah Mountainwater

YULE —WINTER SOLSTICE
Shortest Day, Longest Night—December 20-23
Direction: North

Now this is the solstice
Longest night of the year
Roots - grow from toes
Force through wood and concrete
Anchor us to motherearth
Vines - grow from fingers
Weave woman to woman to woman
This is solstice
Longest night of the year
In darkness we join to wait out this night
The womb of the dark is the birth of the light
Ila Suzanne

Theme:

Celebration of The Night

Goddesses Of Winter Solstice Night:

Mari, Mehen, Belili, Neith, Sarama, Baba Yaga, Ament,
Hakea, Srinmo, Seshat, Nanshe, Ereshkigal.

HERSTORY:

The sun arcs low in the sky, rising and setting at her northern
extreme. At this celebration European pagans lit fires that
burned for seven days, kindled from the remains of the previous

year's Yule log. The ashes were strewn on the fields to ensure fertility. In Northern Europe evergreen trees have always been associated with Yule.

The solar year is an old crone, snug in her hibernation; darkness is all around. The Sun and Earth seem to stand still, the breath of nature is suspended, forces of the nurturing and healing darkness are at work. A live potted tree, which can be planted in the earth after Yule, is part of the ritual circle, or one is decorated outside with lights or ornaments. We honor the Goddess of Life by never cutting down a live tree or purchasing one that has been cut in reverence to the environment. We need all earth's trees, especially now when vast areas of forests are being slaughtered. Removal of too many trees that breathe out precious oxygen needed for human life on the planet will render existence as we know it impossible.

Going into the depths, we womyn, hand-in-hand with our planet, have taken our last inbreath: on Yule we change and begin with the exhaling of the following seasons.

The fire of Yule plays an important role, and mirrors are used to play with reflections from the fire. Some rituals include staying up all night and watching for the dawn, chanting and singing herald in the new day. On this longest night, we renew and rebirth our bodies and spirit selves.

In preparation for Yule we observe a day when we stop all work, stay at home and clean out things we no longer need or want, then put them aside to give to friends or those who need them. This practise was the original basis of gift-giving at this time of year.

The Altar:

The fire is laid, but not lit, in either the woodstove or the cauldron in the middle of the circle.

Boughs of evergreen, holly and mistletoe adorn the room and altar. The evergreen represents the Tree of Life, the Goddess in Her enduring fertility. We lovingly decorate Her branches, and promise to protect our earthmother as we commit ourselves to Her survival and an end to the rape of Her Body.

Suggested Yule Ritual:

Altar and sacred space are prepared, as described above. The circle is cast with bells, purified, and the five directions are addressed. As a magical tool, the rattle is used in this ceremony to shake things up for change. The room is in total darkness and is still. Women enter through the East portal, using the ritual "From Women You Are Born" Chapter 7, or by repeating " I enter this circle in perfect love and perfect trust." This is done quietly with an air of stillness. Womyn then sit in the beautiful darkness, silent for a while, then begin to chant songs to the dark.

**Blessed be the darkness, blessed be the endless night
Blessed be the darkness, hold me like a bird in flight**

Invocation to Yule:

"The darkness is all around us and in us. Blessed Be to the blanket of longest night. We are wrapped in the cave of the crone's winter-womb. So we plant our seeds of change as we leap the fire and wish our dreams. The magic solstice darkness surrounds us".

Each womon has brought a candle and holder, which she places in front of her. Moving doesil, to the left, she sits in her darkness and tells her story of the previous year and what she wishes to change for the coming cycle. Then she lights her candle, saying "I heal and learn in the darkness, I plant my seed of (truth, love, friendship.... whatever is appropriate) for the coming winter season."

When the candles are all burning, the firewoman ignites the already prepared fire, as well as the altar candles. Each womon leaps the fire and speaks a wish. The group repeats her wish out loud two more times, so it is spoken a total of three times.

If the tree has candles, they are lit. With the lighting of her tree candle, each woman gives a prayer for the earth, such as, "I pray to stop the clearcutting of our sacred trees." The group can speak her wish twice more, so the spell is again spoken thrice—"stop the clearcutting." Another might say, "Stop the pollution, may life return to the air," and the womyn repeat, "Stop pollution."

Everyone can put one gift on the tree or in a basket—something she has made, purchased, or traded. These can be distributed later, as each one takes a gift for herself or for a friend who needs it.

We create webs of energy by making material webs of fibers. Within the circle structure we throw balls of cotton, wool, or rayon back and forth, to symbolize catching the sun. Thus the solstice web is formed. While weaving we chant:

**We are the flow, we are the ebb,
We are the weavers, we are the web.
We are the weavers, we are the web,
We are the witches back from the dead.**

by Shekhinah Mountainwater

Warm food is passed around, each woman feeding the one to her left, saying, "May you never hunger." We can also pass warm drink around, saying, "May you never thirst."

Other songs/chants can be sung. The cone of power is raised and sent to the earth. The Circle is closed, directions thanked. Feasting and merriment continue.

WINTER SOLSTICE STORY

The daylight was bleak, with grey clouds blanketing the sky over the ocean. The winter sea wore her ashen mantle as she drew in her last breath of the season. We'd asked The Mother for "no fog", and its absence was surely a miracle in the middle of winter.

About twelve o'clock women began arriving for the Yule gather. By two's and three's they came to celebrate; by mid-afternoon there were twelve of us and we decided to begin. We lamented we were only twelve, until we realized that a very charming and active little dog, companion of a womon present, was the thirteenth.

It wasn't too cold outside so we gathered on the headlands, as close to the ocean as we could get. Initially, we stood in a circle, but it didn't feel right for half of us to have our backs to Her, so we rearranged in a crescent moon facing the sea. The womyn on both ends agreed to hold hands with the ocean.

Twelve years later and I still remember that day as if looking into a precious clear crystal. Baba was on my right; I held the ocean's hand on the left.

We cast the circle, purified with cedar and sage, and invoked the directions with "Oh, Crone of Darkness, send us your wisdom, healing and nurturing." After that I can't remember exactly what was said or what Goddesses were invoked; it isn't important now. I do remember the stillness, the grayness, the feeling of the day. When it became time to raise the cone of power, we began by calling Goddesses of the Night, and then the **"Ma"** chant began. It took off like a bird in flight, carrying the energy higher and higher as the powerful cone rose before us. We were all deeply in trance. I saw one or two womyn out of the corner of my eye, all of us locked in ecstasy. The heat was rising where I held Baba's hand. So strong was the energy link, I felt that our hands might begin to burn. I can't quite believe that she's dead now.

Just as the cone was about to peak I could feel an intense brightness on my eyelids. I opened my eyes to see the clouds parting as if the whole sky was opening up before us! The splendor of those sacred rays of pure glistening gold streaming into the ocean from the blue-grey clouds made me gasp. The entire sky around us on three sides was illuminated with Her glory.

I revelled in the beauty before me, and as I stood transfixed, a bevy of about a dozen or so whales began swimming in figure-eight formations towards the shore, bathing in that healing and magical solstice energy.

It was so splendid, and we were all so deeply touched by Her magnificence that tears poured down our faces—tears of joy and love for Our Mother Ocean and an intense yearning love for the whales. We were mesmerized. The chanting went on and on. Time was lost as we entered a place beyond time. The whales slowly swam in circles raising their heads out of the water in ecstasy. Out of the dark mother's womb, a solstice birth was happening; birth of this profound and wonderful interspecies communication; and rebirth of parts of ourselves, for there was not a womon among us who was not deeply changed.

The chanting finally peaked, and we sent the energy cone to the whales, thanking them for this honor, born of incredible trust. As the sky began to close and dress herself in the gray robe She had worn before Her revelation, the whales began their journey back out to the sea. Soon our chanting was but a whisper.

It was now late afternoon and darkness was descending into the longest night: we welcomed Her with love. We stood there a while in the silence of our inner stillness, then closed the ritual circle. We had been midwives in the creation of the light and had planted seeds for a new dawn.

This is a true story.

**BRIGHID, BRIDE, IMBOLC, OIMELC, ST. BRIGID'S EVE,
BRIGHID, FEAST OF THE FLAME, CANDLEMAS
February 1-2
Direction - East**

First of the four Cross-Quarter Holydays
Midpoint between Winter Solstice and Vernal Equinox
Waxing Light, Sun-warmed Earth, Groundhog Day

Circle of wimmin, halfway to spring
Quickening hope, earthsoul rising
Candlemas song to waxing light
Bridget's fire burning bright

Cauldron, broom, candle, wine
Apple, Elder, Dogwood, Pine
New witch, old witch, spiral line
Circle of womyn, circle of time
                    Ila Suzanne

Theme:

Initiation, Purification

Goddesses of Brigit:

Brigit—Goddess of fire, inspiration, healing,
childbirth, poets, smithys, craftswimmin;
Cerridwen—Goddess of the Cauldron and fortress of wisdom;
Dana—Goddess who has total command of fire and water;
Inari—Goddess of Fire and Smithcraft;
Imanja (Brazil—Goddess of Februa (meaning purification).

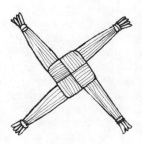

The firewheel (pictured above) represents the hands of The
Goddess giving gifts. The radial arms represent the four
phases of the moon; the center being the place where all
energy meets.

HERSTORY:

"Brighid (Candlemas) is the time of year to make a
commitment or recommitment to your spiritual growth. I find it
interesting that this time of the year is also Valentine's Day—the
day to show love for someone. Of course, at one time these two
days were the same and celebrated as one.

"Brighid was a mighty Celtic Triple Goddess, patron of artists,
craftswimmin and healers, known for her cauldron of
transformation. She was famous for her love of poor folk. Once
her father tried to marry her off because he couldn't afford
Brighid constantly giving away his property when she found
someone cold or hungry. The two of them drove off in a fine
carriage to arrange the wedding and while he was talking to the
prospective groom Brighid sold the horse and carriage to feed
the poor. The groom decided he didn't want to marry her after all,
so she lived unwedded and happy, never cured of her
compassion. And her followers became known for a passion, for
social justice, and would heal rich and poor alike, and stood
always with those who were fighting for their homes and

families. When the monks came to Ireland, they forced Brighid's followers to change from their white robes of joy to more somber ones, but the nuns tend the sacred fire of St. Brighid to this day."[4]

"It was not until the patriarchal religions came along did we start thinking of loving feelings and commitment to the higher power as two different things. Then commitment came to mean suffering and sacrifice and not the joyous feeling of being in total accord with all that is. One of the ways we can trace Valentines Day to Candlemas is through the use of the color red. Candlemas is when we burn red candles to symbolize the passion that is felt and expressed at the time of commitment. It is a time to understand the power and the powerfulness that is felt once you give up your Ego in surrender. Surrender does **not** mean the surrender into suffering that was a hallmark of the Christian martyrs, but one of letting go of the Ego and getting in touch with your essence; that very spark of life that keeps you moving on your path, learning, growing and becoming.

"If you are new to the celebrations of wimmin's spirituality, use Brigit to initiate yourself into the mysteries of life. If you have been celebrating this day for years, use the passion of red energy to recommit yourself to your spiritual path, the path of self-knowledge and fearless action."[5]

This is a European festival of the beginning of spring, to coax the sun's return and bring an end to the cold weather. Rituals focus on fertility, purification and initiation. It was the custom on Brighid's eve to make a "Brighid's Bed" of hay in a place near the door. In it is placed a figure of grain or corn sheaves dressed as a woman. All night long, females of the household sat up and kept a torch burning to energize the corn woman. They channelled the fertilizing powers of the moon to give the people a successful planting and harvest.

Like most ancient festivals, it began at the preceding moonrise when every candle and lamp was lit. Fires burned in all the hearths and outside bonfires blazed. Brighid's fires are lit with the last of the dry Yule greenery kept for that purpose: every womon contributes something to the fire as a token of a clean sweep and new beginnings. A new broom, decked with ribbon streamers, had the same significance. Paper birds were burned to symbolize Goddess offerings for each other's health, happiness and prosperity. Old flames were extinguished and new ones lit at nightfall. Brighid's celebration was to encourage the sun's swift return and to bring an end to winter. In Scandanavia crowns of lighted candles adorned the heads of celebrants and merry choruses coaxed the sun closer to grace us with Her light. Brighid hails spring.

Her sacred fire has always been tended by the daughters of the flame and only women were allowed to see it. This holyday is also called "feast of the candles" (Candlemas), "feast of lights", or "feast of the flame". St. Brigid is the Christianized form of Brigentis, Bride or Briid, also called Cerridwen. We celebrate the emergence of the sun as well as the rebirth of the moon. It is the day when we look towards spring, turning the wheel once more.

At Brighid the waxing sun begins to warm the earth. We begin to dry out from the rains and the groundhog comes out of her hole to check the progress, our assurance that winter will end and spring will arrive. This Sabbat honors the moon as source of fertility for the months to come. New witches are initiated on this fire festival when the still winter world reawakens and first feels the quickening of life. The days grow longer. It is a time of changes below the surface of things, when solstice births first begin to manifest.

It is traditional to make candles, some of them from last year's recycled working candles. Candlemaking can be done during the day of the Brighid ritual and the candles used in the evening.

The Altar:
White or Red Cloth, gold or silver candles, a corn doll

Suggested Ritual:

Circle is opened, directions addressed. On Brigid, new witches are initiated and take their "magic" names. Old Witches rededicate themselves to the Goddess and The Craft.

The ritual is begun with purification, and an indoor hottub is a good place to do this, if it is available. A hot bath can be substituted. If dandelion blossoms, Brigit's flowers, are available, they can be sprinkled on the water.

The womon (or wimmin) wishing initiation—and she (they) must ask the group for it, comes to the ritual in only a robe. She brings a set of clothes which symbolize The Craft to her. The womon who has agreed to vouch for her brings the nine-foot braided red witch's cord.

A cauldron containing sand is set in the middle of the circle; one candle burns in it: the first candle is lit on Brigid by the Priestess, possibly a newly-formed candle made earlier in the day when the wimmin have gathered to dip candles.

The corn doll is brought to the circle and put in a basket with fresh greenery for her bed. The prayer pipe or rattle is passed, opening Brigid with a prayer.

All wimmin move around the purification water. Initiates, one by one, remove their robes and dip in the water, repeating:

"I purify and bless myself with this water. I have studied The Craft of the Wise a year and a day and I am committed to perpetuating the teachings."

As each womon emerges from the water, she is dried and passed through a birth canal formed by the womyn's legs. (Z. Budapest suggests pulling her through on a sheepskin rug). If possible, she can be passed through a canal of locked arms.

When she emerges on the other end of this canal, she is welcomed with kisses, affirmations and "welcome, sister" by the initiated witches. She steps into her new clothing.

Priestess:
"Who vouches for this womon?"
Initiated group member Answers:
"I vouch for this woman, that she has studied the teachings of The Goddess for a year and a day." (Or however long she has, but that must be the minimum time)
Priestess asks the following questions:
"Are you ready to commit yourself to The Goddess?"
"What is your chosen magical name?"
"What do you promise?"
"What are your goals for the coming year?"
When she has given her answers, she is presented with a flower wreath for her hair and her nine-foot braided cord is wrapped around her.
Priestess:
"This is your witch's girdle. Feel the strength of your promises. This cord will bind your promises and protect you. You stand at the crossroads once again. This is a moment of major change in your life."
The new witch lights a candle from the solitary burning one and places it in the cauldron.

Old witches may choose to rededicate themselves at this time. After speaking her recommitment to the group, she lights a candle, places it in the cauldron, and makes her promise to Brigid's cauldron. If you work alone, you may chose to rededicate yourself at Brigit.

This is the night of the Muse. Storytelling, songs, dances are offered to Brigit, "the fairy arrow". Instruments are played. Libations are given, sunflower sprouts are fed to each other, a symbol of the newness and delicacy of this Sabbat and of the life force.

The rattle is passed. The circle is closed and the feast begins. Brigit loves good parties, so make this a great one!

Blessed Be.

Invocation to Brigit:

Be with us Brighid, mighty Celtic Triple Goddess of the flame and the flood, crafts, weaving and creativity. You who bring inspiration, healing, art, poetry, medicine, smithcraft, be with your sisters tonight.   Stir the cauldron of ideas and transformation.

Mistress of the Muse, you who heal the sick, fire the spark of inspiration in our souls so we may create sacred art forms in Your name. Bless our creative juices that we may bring beauty to the world.

Come to us with air, creating words and thoughts,
Come to us with fire for the potter's kiln, the smithy's forge,
Come to us with water to heal the sick with love and compassion,
Come to us with earth and bless our creations, born at solstice, now to manifest.

BRIGIT STORY—THE WEATHER

The weather is having hard times. April in January, July in April—parched clay soil, scorched tiny spring sprout blossoms, their little flower heads bowed and wilting in the heat. Whether we like it or not, drought has come.

Today, there was rain, the glorious, refreshing, life-giving wonder of wet, slippery, soggy rain. I've never been so thankful for it! Our weather's in trouble—the planet's protection has been severely damaged and this influences the weather. No buffer zone from the sun, no earth blanket. The ozone is disappearing. "Ain't nowhere you can run, no, no, no."

Drought; the name brings fear to us humans who are composed of 95% water. In the past, we could generally predict the seasons and weather changes—no more. Whether we like it or not, weather remains unpredictable. Planning is virtually impossible.

Can you weather the storms? Can you weather the heat is a more pertinent question. Can you weather this life—full of roller coaster dizzying curves, steep breathtaking plunges, then upswings, like the weather? Can you survive everything going wrong? Health in crisis? A drought? Drought of the soul, drought of the personality? I am experiencing a drought, personally and internally. Rain is overdue. I don't want small showers that last a day or half-day, or an hour. I want full-tilt boogie **rain** pounding on my roof—north wind blows—trees sway, thunder claps, lightning flashes, give it to us!   We wait, just as I wait for my change, my upswing, on the rise, full-blown life happiness again, doors opening, spirit expanding; and more rain. And I got it........

ANOTHER BRIGIT STORY—THE STORM

The storm is all-consuming—the rain pours without stop from the sky, gushing sheets, yes, walls of water. As I dig the trench I become aware of a giant stream of water penetrating my thin plastic coat. I shiver and pray for immunity from all cold-like diseases. At last I lift the last bit of mud onto my shovel and a miracle begins—the water rushes wildly through the small trench, running and racing on her journey to the creek. I am filled with satisfaction, knowing that I have been instrumental in providing a channel, knowing I am part of all this; not removed, not a fearful spectator of the Mother's greatest show I have seen yet in my ten years in the country and on the land; being part of The Storm, the 9986 California flood.

The steep and winding half-mile road into our land has to be checked several times a day, top and bottom. Two mud slides so far. All the trenches must be kept open or the house could flood because it sits at the bottom of a valley of hills. An act of faith. Staying here is now declared an act of faith in the Goddess. The Seven Sisters, protective oaks of my home, sway in the strong, ferocious wind.

At night we burn the candles. Red for survival and the first chakra, yellow and gold for the Sun altar we have set in the South, with the bright and glowing yellow cloth, along with two Magical Crystals and Daughters of the Moon tarot cards painted by us, representing the Sun. We pray for the earth to take what She needs and then for the rain to stop.

Sometimes I feel the panic rolling in, like a menacing cloud of doom, panic that the storm will go on forever, long past the time we can survive it. There are constant warnings on the radio. Floods, rivers of water, and roads closed (ours certainly is). The Russian River floods, Guerneville is under water. Helicopters evacuate people; death, injuries, mud slides burying houses and people. The mud keeps sliding down our hills too, and here we sit, in our valley, high hills on all sides: hills of clay, mud, sand and soft earth. Water rages everywhere and the creek swells to a small, fast-moving river, loud, swift and muddy.

We remember the predictions of the Hopi, the psychics, astrologers, the wise ones, that the time has arrived. The predictions say that during this time when many planets are transiting the sign of Scorpio and bringing the energy of Transformation, Death and Rebirth, this civilization as we know it will cease to exist. It will be destroyed by a series of natural disasters for the purification of Mother Earth in order for her to survive the devastation of this planet, her holy body. I do understand that She needs to clean Herself of the pollution, trash and poison, and these disturbances are her natural ways of doing that.

We move downstairs as our upstairs bedroom is too loud to sleep in, due to the roar of the water. There is a small part of me that is a frightened child who doesn't trust that I will be cared for in all this, that maybe I will die. Or will I have to leave here if that is what it takes to survive? Could I leave my home after working a lifetime to find a place where I can stay and grow old and then pass on to the next world in peace? To stay or to go—it is a weighty decision that we must discuss, two womyn out here alone with The Storm. Another part of me thinks that if I need to die for the purification of the Earth, my Mother, then I will gladly go, surrendering my body so She can disperse the poison and become clean again.

I come back to the present, here, now in my body, lifting the shovel of mud and getting thoroughly soaked as I dig the ditch. There is something to be said for getting really soaked—to the bone, through layers of cloth and plastic... wet.... soaked..... sogged..... sometimes it's wonderful and gratifying. Renate, my love, who also calls this place home, is running madly down the road, dancing with the wild oaks, madrones, and tall graceful pines, all twirling wildly in the storm. She howls with the wind. The dog joins in, then so do I. The goats hear the sounds and start Ma-ing the chorus; Lola with her deep voice and Magnolia Truffle, the pygmy goat, with her small, high one. The Goat Mothers, Trudy and Rosa, are busy demolishing the lower-level bowels of the house, their new home since the goat barn was flooded. They amuse themselves by sharpening their horns on the posts and charging back and forth, smashing into the cornerposts. They provide the conga beat and the frogs sing their chant every time the rain stops. We are a country orchestra, and the sound of the earth is loud and clear as we hear her pain and joy. And we, in our menagerie, develop the trust that makes it possible to stay on this tiny piece of earth and be thankful for what we have.

SPRING EQUINOX - VERNAL EQUINOX
March 20-23
Direction: East

Winter is behind us
Gai—Mother Earth calls her daughters' dancing
feet to her warming mountain thighs
Feel her sweet sap running in bones and spirit
Persephone, Inanna, Kore
The maidens in us rise
Demeter, Astarte, Cerridwen
Our motherselves cradle
Our own young souls
As spring is born again
                                        Ila Suzanne

Theme:

Rebirth, Change

Goddesses of Spring Equinox:

Demeter, Persephone, Nepthys, Freya, Flora, Blodeuwedd,
Eostre, the Maiden Goddess (Easter), Damara-ana and Ishtar,
Goddesses of Fertility. Menvra and Cupra wield their
thunderbolts.

HERSTORY:

Vernal Equinox is the halfway point between winter and the bright, advancing tide of summer. The traditional fertility festival, Eostre (Easter), was to celebrate the Virgin Goddesses, rebirth of the Earth, and make magic for her fruitfulness. The word Easter comes from Eostra or Oestre, Goddess of fertility, known in early Briton. The hare and the scarlet egg are sacred symbols of regenerative power. During Oestre's festival, hot cross buns are eaten; their origin is symbolic of the yoni or vulva.

Spring Equinox, in the sign of Aries, is one of the two points of balance on the Wheel of the Year in the Northern Hemisphere. The other point occurs in the sign of Libra, at Fall Equinox. All over the world there is equal day and night, dark and light in balance.

This is the time of the rosy-cheeked maiden, of rebirth, when Aries sparks the firepower spirit of youth inside each womon. The seeds of Yule and Bridgit manifest as action and matter. With the Spring, we look to the East, to dawn. The power of the sea, rainmaking, courting the flash of lightning. There is the blessing of fields. It is the season when plants awaken and first buds burst into bloom, seeds sprout, the buzz of insects fill the air with their music, tadpoles are born, the sap flows, and earth opens fully to new life energy and wakes in wonder as she becomes fertile again. Flowers smile and open; lupen, narcissus, daffodils, tulips, cherry blossoms, and crocus bring the glorious colors of spring. Pussy willows peak their furry faces to the sun as sap pulses its silent music through the veins of trees. The tide pulls at our passions, our bodies, love flows into us, everything is pulsating with new life.

Equinox is a midpoint between the inwardness of winter and the outer energy of summer. Spring marks the reunion of Persephone and Demeter (she is Kore while in the underworld, and Persephone, when she returns in the spring). Persephone dances with Demeter, children rejoice with the playfulness of nymphs, mothers and daughters everywhere reunite. The continuance between mothers and daughters is celebrated as separations dissolve, in the season of children's joy and laughter, vitality, vibrancy, and wild pleasures.

Eggs are the universal symbol of life—the cosmic egg symbol appears in creation myths all over the world. Spring is celebrated by honoring Oestre, Goddess of the egg and the hare. At Spring Equinox we paint eggs half in dark colors and half in light, to symbolize the balance of dark moontime and solar light.

The Ash is the tree of Spring Equinox, a tree of magic, the Goddess' tree of justice. Womyn feel wild, unhampered by the cold weather and pleasure takes priority. With the beauty of the season comes a fierce love of the Earth and new vows to help protect what sacred beauties are still left for us. We know we can always begin again in spring, and each time, we are older and wiser.

This is the Direction of the East, the season of beginnings. The rhythm of life picks up, we spring-clean our closets, altars and psyches, and dust the cobwebs from our house and mind. I marvel at life around me; there is renewed hope for change.

THE ALTAR:

It is set with intensely colored cloths and green candles, symbolizing the return of green to the earth. Spring flowers, especially wild ones, crocus, pussy willow, daffodils, trilliums, are in abundance. If eggs have been painted, they can be displayed on the altar for all to see (and later eat). Seeds, bread, apples, nuts and pomegranate seeds are included, to be empowered by the circle energy.

Suggested Ritual for Spring Equinox:

The circle is opened, purified, and the directions are called using a spring flower held up to each direction.

Priestess: "We spark the spirit of the Maiden within us, the fire power of Aries."

Wimmin dance around the burning fire, holding branches with ribbons attached, which they later will throw in the fire. The spiral dance can be performed, or this could also be a renaming ritual or planting seeds in the garden.

The Priestess repeats the chant, over and over, until the energy is high:

**Mother, daughter, sister, lover, hear us, hear us,
It is you we seek within us, Goddess, Goddess**

The group begins a **Ma** chant. When it peaks and the cone of power is formed, the Priestess asks that the energy raised is sent for renewal of the earth and rebirth of maiden energy in each womon.

Everyone then sits around the circle taking turns speaking(to the left), sharing stories of mothers, daughters and grandmothers. We can also paint eggs while chanting and singing. Sunflower and alfalfa sprouts are passed around and fed to the womon on the left, repeating "Eat the live food of spring. May you never hunger."

When the storytelling is finished, recorded drum music can be played or if there are any accomplished drummers, they begin to drum for the dancing. The drums throb, stronger and stronger, the dancing gets wilder and wilder. The Priestess calls out, "Spring is bursting!", "The Maiden returns!", or "The Earth is Alive!".

Invocation to Spring:

"The wheel of change spins round to spring again. It is time to change and begin again. Rejoice in Spring, for the Maiden, the first aspect of The Goddess, returns!"

Spring is the season of Eostre, She who opens the gates and offers up spring, birthing us once more. It is the time of balance between winter and summer solstice: dusk and dawn are aligned in the harmony of the Equinox. The greyness of winter fades in the distance. Persephone lifts her innocent face to the sun.

Each womon gives a prayer of thanks for life and counts her blessings out loud. The fire is kindled as the firewomon lights the cauldron or outdoor fire, then the altar candles.

SPRING EQUINOX STORY
FIRST BLOODS (MENARCHE)

I felt the sticky wetness flowing out of me and dripping down my leg, and I knew that it was the beginning of my first bloods. I had been enlightened by the members of my tribe about what would happen, but one thing I intuitively knew was that this sacred time would have deep implications on my life. It was my coming of age, a commitment to my womonhood, and also a time of budding sexuality and passion—the magical age of 13; I remember it well. I knew the magic of the moment—this springtime—would never happen again in my entire life, so I knew I must hold the moment and rejoice in it.

Yara was waiting as I came home from my work of planting gardens with the other children. As I burst in the door our eyes met, and held, as I beamed a slow smile at her. "Yara, it's happened," I said with excitement. She ran to me, and held me fast to her breast. "I'm so happy. Sit down, let me get you some tea. I'll call the other mothers, and we'll plan your bloods celebration for the Spring Equinox, just three days from now. You will have to inform the garden crew that you can't work until after your passage. We must prepare for the ritual; then you will be instructed further by the mothers."

I was excited to know that I would receive my new name, knowledge of what womonhood meant, my favorite foods, and many gifts. As I sat in a snug corner next to the woodstove, Yara gathered clean clothes and a special handmade belt she had woven just for this occasion. I felt a little woozy and unstable for the first time since my blood had come, but Yara, my present year-mother, bid me lay down and handed me a cup of Saint Joan's Wort tea, gathered by the tribal wimmin every Summer Solstice to be used for menstrual toning and cramps. It felt so good and warm in my belly, so relaxing and nurturing.

For three days I was in seclusion to prepare for initiation into the coven. I listened to the mothers who taught me the blood mysteries and I also listened to my own heartbeat. I dreamed of my new name and chanted silently and out loud. I was given a book to record my dreams and told that they were very special. I ate very little, cleansing myself with water. I became a wemoon.

The wimmin gathered for my initiation in the early morning of Spring Equinox by a running stream in the forest. There was a special pool in the stream, lined with rocks. I sat meditating by it while I waited for the womyn of our village to arrive. When they did, I slowly took off my dress and laid out the clay bowl, shaped like a vulva, full of my first menstrual blood. My 13 mothers stepped forward, each dipped her fingers in my blood and painted my naked body. When they were done I stepped into the sparkling water of the small pool while the wimmin sang to me and tossed spring wildflowers over my painted body. The water felt so wonderfully clean and refreshing on my skin: I was beginning to feel sticky and ripe after three days and the water truly cleansed my body and soul. The chanting and singing grew to full volume and filled up my senses; as I totally immersed myself in the wildflower-strewn water. My mothers, who had each nurtured me for one year of my life, stepped forward and formed a ring around me as I floated there. Each mother washed me with sweet-smelling soap. One washed my hair, one my face, another my feet, arms, legs, all over, with love. They then sat and waited for me on the edge of the pool, and as I emerged, I was dried, then anointed with sweet warm almond oil by each and helped into my new blood-red dress. My mothers pinned the 13 roses, one from each of them, in my black hair and on my bodice.

The power circle was formed in a clearing in the forest. The thirteen blood mothers stood in the inner circle with the elders while the village womyn made ever-widening circles around them. There were five circles in all. The muted sunlight of morning streamed down through the redwoods with a pink light—a magical sacred space. I stood outside the circle and when it was opened and purified I spoke:

"I was born a womon of wimmin

Gifted with the wonder, knowledge and understanding of wimmin

I feel a glorious change in me

As I accept new responsibilities and make conscious choices for my life

Knowing that a moment's passion and an ongoing life commitment
Are two different things
Help me to keep my pledges with loving teaching
Nurture me in my love of The Goddess
Harbor my soul.'

(Above quote By Norma Joyce and Ffiona Morgan)

The wimmin chant, "Come join our wimmin's circle in full knowledge. We welcome you and your energy."
Their hands opened to welcome me. I light the three red candles on the center altar and with each one I chant:
"I light this candle for my sister/mother the moon
For now we are one with our cycles,
I light this candle for my mother, the Earth;
For now I can feel her roots and eternal nature.
I light this candle for my moon sign of Capricorn, and personal Goddess, Medea, my astrological affinity and guardian".
The Priestess asks "Who offers this Maiden?"
My 13 mothers answer: "We offer her in love to the Goddess."
As I finished lighting the candles a chant began and the cone of power was raised. The Priestess sent the cone in a waterfall back down on me, for my health, happiness and prosperity. A tunnel of mothers was formed, oldest to youngest, and my new name was chanted as I was passed from womon to womon in this ritual of rebirth. The Priestess sings,

"Blessed child, now a womon,
From wimmin you are born into this world
From wimmin you are born into this circle.'

Each of the village wimmin has made me a first-bloods gift of something red, and after the birth canal ritual was finished I received them. One of them was a bloodstone in a medicine bag. We then passed around the red apples, cakes and other red goodies, feeding each other and repeating "May you never hunger.....May you never thirst.' The circle was closed.

If it wasn't for the wimmin, wimmin
We would not be living, living
We would not be joyful, singing
Loved and beloved. . . wimmin.
                                             Alix Dobkin

**BELTANE (Celtic meaning "Bright Fire"),
MAY EVE , ROODMAS
April 30 - May 1st
Direction: South**

Beltane Song

Sappha Rauni Bona Dea
Flora Vesta Aphrodite
Danu Maia Seronia
Come Lady May to Beltane fires
Where Maiden Earth so ripe is waiting
Dance the music of your desires
Jump the flames, toss the flowers
Search out honey-scented bowers
Find the altar to the Maiden
Drink Her nectar, taste Her bread
Lay Her down on earth's warm bed
Light more fires, jump more flames
Come Lady May to Beltane games
Sappha Rauni Bona Dea
Flora Vesta Aphrodite
Danu Maia Seronia
                    Ila Suzanne

Theme: Passion

Goddesses:

Olwyn May Queen; Spider Woman; Brigid, The Fairy Queen; Maia, Goddess of Increase; Flora, Flower Goddess of leaf and stem, branch and blossom; Aphrodite-Love; Vesta and Her Virgins; Bona Dea,Goddess of Healing; Rauni; Sappha, symbol of women's love; Lada, Goddess of Spring.

HERSTORY:

"Beltane is the midpoint between Spring Equinox and Summer Solstice. This is one of the four ancient fire festivals of Europe, also called the 'Power Gates', which contain the fixed zodiacal signs. The sign of Beltane is the Power Gate of the Earth element. There is a focused release of earth energy, the beginning of an elemental power tide and the full potential of the earth."[6]

Flowers open at Beltane. The children make flower wreaths to wear and garlands of flowers adorn the wimmin's houses in celebration of this festival. It is opposite Samhain (All Hallows) on the wheel. Samhain is the time when the veil between the worlds is thinnest, and Beltane the time when the worlds are furthest apart.

Today lovers play and love together. On this day we celebrate the May Queen of fertility and passion, a time when the Maiden of Spring Equinox comes of age and celebrates the fullness of her sexuality, dancing sky-clad (nude) in the fields to ensure a good harvest. Wimmin open themselves in intimacy and dance the maypole outdoors to welcome summer. They leap the bonfires at night with friends and lovers. The maypole, symbol of the Tree of Life or Moon Tree, is decorated with flowers and ribbons that are attached to the top. Thanks is given for the Abundance of Spring.

"In medieval France, May was the month of women. It was marked by all manner of rites of reversal, with women on top in all the daily patriarchal power rituals. Husbands who continued to beat and berate their wives could expect to be shiboreed, something like tarred and feathered and paraded through town on a donkey by the local masking society. Pater-families who were miserly and puritanical through other seasons were expected to wax generous, tolerant, and playful, as the womenfolk tuned in to the greening of the earth, forsaked their work, went a maying, danced the maypole, and engaged in a sprinkling for the May Queen. We celebrate the coming of age of the Maiden Goddess on May Eve."[7]

"Beltane, May Day, or Roodmas falls on the first of May and is another of the spring festivals of fecundity and the moon, with special emphasis on the living spirit of vegetation, newly awakened in spring. In Briton its eve is called Walpurgis Nacht, and special emphasis is placed on rituals of protecting oneself from the evils of others. The fires of Walpurgis Nacht are called Beltane, still the Gaelic word for May. Huge bonfires were kindled on hills after which a large meal was prepared. When they had finished, they sang and danced around the fire in a ring. They leaped over the glowing coals or even through the flames. Towards the end of the gathering a large cake was brought out, baked with eggs and scalloped around the edge, called the Beltane cake. Pieces were broken off and given to each one. May Day and our month were named after the ancient roman Goddess Maia, meaning 'to increase'.

"On her day, folks rose early and went 'a-maying' in the woods to the sound of music to gather flowers and greenery for garlands and gifts. Garlanded revelers went from door to door singing and were given gifts to insure prosperity of the householder in the year to come. Sometimes the singers were accompanied by one womon completely covered in leaves, called the Leafy One or the Leaf Queen, to represent the spirit of vegetation.

"The Maypole or Maytree was a straight green tree, an embodiment of the tree spirit, or spirit of vegetation. It was brought from the woods with much ceremony. Its lower branches were removed, its trunk smoothed, and was set up in a public place. Its top was left green and fresh above the ribbon streamers and garlands of flowers with which it was decked. Perhaps even more powerful would be an uncut living tree, tall and limbless to a fair height, the ribbons attached just above or below its lower branches.

"Such a tree in the woods would be the center for the day's maying festivities, including of course, the Maypole dance. Each dancer takes the end of one streamer and dances around the tree, thereby interweaving the ribbons, symbolic of bright colored leaves, flowers and fruit, all gifts of the moon goddess, giver of fertility."[8]

The Altar:

Fruits, greenery, spring flowers, green and other bright candles, bowls of fruit, nuts, cakes, and jugs of sweet cherry, peach, and apricot juice. Breads, fruit, Hawthorne branches.

Suggested Ritual:

Open the Circle, purify, call the Directions, and burn the herb Artemesia. Tonight, we rub our bodies with herbs, flowers and plants, to smell sweet, then bless each other with water. As we dance the maypole ribbon dance (see below), we joyously weave our connectedness as wimmin; the webs of our lives and loves. Music is chanted or played—the music of spring. Bells, rattles, and drums are played to celebrate the season of flowering. Green is the color of Beltane, the color of the fresh green earth.

Invocation to Beltane:

"Queen of the May, Flora, Goddess of leaf and stem, branch and blossom, open your gates of passion for us, your lovers. You who bring desire, fertility, life, who are the soul of wildness, bless us with roses, kiss us with iris."

We plant our garden, blessing the seeds. If your garden is already growing, the small plants can be blessed. We form a circle to dance the spiral and turn the wheel, lightly kissing as we pass—wild selves meeting wild selves. We shed our shirts dancing by the fire, some wimmin dance sky-clad, wearing only necklaces, shells, herbs, flowers in the hair. We hold green ribbons and jump the bonfire for purification: on Beltane we have a bright fire.

"The Great Rite is sexual license, "when we act out the lovemaking of nature by loving each other, we heal ourselves of all lost love. We writhe like snakes, uncoiling our desire. We open the gates of intimacy. We release love relationships and love wishes into the fire of love."9

Directions for the Maypole Dance

The Maypole or tree must stand on its own and be sturdy. Form a circle, far out from the pole, with alternate wimmin facing different directions. Each one holds a long ribbon, pulled taut, that she has attached to the top of the Maypole. There should be an even number of dancers.

When the music begins, wimmin move in the directions they are facing, passing right shoulders with the first and left shoulders with the next. The ribbons are braided around the Maypole. Those passing on the inside will have to duck, and those passing on the outside will have to raise their ribbons.

MAY EVE STORY:
BELTANE LOVERS

It was the night of the Great Rite and time to drink the powerful brew. They were all waiting for me—my lovers, my sisters. Today we had danced the maypole together, laughing and singing in our joyous celebration of life. Now it was nighttime, we waited to enjoy The Great Rite.

I had dressed earlier by candlelight, after first washing my body in a salt bath for purification, then in the clear, sweet water from the well. My indigo velvet robe draped my rich, wide hips and my round breasts that blossomed up from the soft, slippery fabric. I brushed my hair until it glistened like spun silk—its many colors of red, brown and gold shone in the candlelit mirrors. Today I had picked a rose for my hair, an iris for the altar, and some lavender for the lovers' bed.

In silence, I tip the silver chalice to my lips tasting the magic herbal potion that will loosen my limbs and fire my passion. It tastes good; both sweet and sour at once. I am almost ready.

Sitting at my altar, candles blazing in the night, I look outside the window at the stars and a sliver of new moon. The night twinkles her greeting. I know it is time, and I admit I am nervous facing the unknown. As I descend the stairs I see the coven gather: tonight all nine of us are here.

Rowina greets me with a kiss and I enter the sacred ritual space. The circle opens and we journey between the worlds. Lorna fires the candles, bringing light into the summer night. I am Priestess and I chant:

We are now between the worlds
The Goddess welcomes her lovers
Hail Sappho, Aphrodite, Oshun, Venus,
All lovers everywhere
Join us now

I am beginning to feel all the tension flow out of my body. The herbal Yohimbe potion is relaxing my fears, easing my worries, preparing me for communion with my sisters. As Priestess I must go first, even though I would rather go last.

I lay in the middle of the circle on the soft velvet bed strewn with flowers and sweet-smelling herbs. They intoxicate me. I am undressed by my lovers, gently, each one kissing a different part of my body as they bare my skin to the fragrant night air. The warm lavender oil is brought from the altar and sixteen hands massage my legs, arms, throat, face, feet, stroking sensually, deliciously, warming all my intimate parts, reaching into all the crevices and canyons of my body. They fondle, then suck my full breasts. My nipples become erect, jutting, straining against their mouths. My sex is aroused by them, as they open the direct line from breast to yoni, clear and strong it pulses. So many hands and mouths; they bring my body higher and higher—I am aware of my clitoris throbbing under the rhythmic caress of a tongue, first slowly, then faster and faster. I strain against the beautiful mouths, tongues and hands of my lovers. The throbbing heat of the sex takes me on a journey that blots out all thought with its passion. I speak, "Yes, oh yes, don't stop". I am hot, so hot with desire, I think my skin must be burning. They love me with words, "Lover, Priestess, Beautiful One, We love you, we want you". I feel another lover's fingers enter my warm wet cave, so wet, so very wet—I am dripping. I moan in ecstasy as they beat the drum sound of love against my walls. Another's mouth is on my pearl, two others suck my breasts. It's almost more than my body can bear, this ecstasy. Faster and faster I move, like a horse galloping across the heavens. I call to Sappho, I reach to the stars and grasp a fiery planet. They chant my name, over and over. I am enveloped by hot flesh, sweet smells, the soft skin and silken hair of women. The cone of power is raised—my body pushes her limits. I bring her to the edge, then explode in a thousand stars, throbbing, throbbing. I cry out, and it fills the room. My molecules rearrange themselves into another pattern.

I lay this way for what seems like forever, in a circle of arms, being held, sung to, rocked by my sisters. One woman lays her cheek on my breast, lovingly holding it close. I touch her velvet cheek, run my hands over her waiting skin, then spark the dance of her body.

It begins again; this time I give rather than receive. We strum the strings of her harp, continuing The Great Rite of Beltane. Another woman lays on top of her and their legs part, welcoming each other into the magic circle of their bodies. They begin to move together, rubbing in pleasure their entire lengths, while I fondle her breasts and the others pleasure her in other ways. We will continue to love like this until every woman has been fully satisfied, fully loved. Beltane night. Night of Love. Night of the Goddess of sexual passion, beloved of Sappho. **All acts of love and pleasure are her rituals**.

This is not a true story and the names have not been
changed to protect the guilty

SUMMER SOLSTICE—MIDSUMMER—LITHA,
Longest Day, Shortest Night
June 20-22
Direction: South

Sing and spin, sing and spin
Half year out, half year in
Earth at full must spiral in
Summer solstice longest light
Burn all fears this brief night
Fairy wheels now start again
Sing and spin, sing and spin
Ila Suzanne

Theme:

Fulfillment, Fortune, Play

Goddesses:

Li (Chinese Goddess of Midsummer)
Oraea, (Goddess of Summer Solstice,)
Cardea, (Goddess of the four Cardinal Winds and The Hinge)
Hestia and Heartha, (Goddesses of the home)
Litha, (Fire Queen of Love)
Artemis, (Goddess of wild places and animals).
Imanja, Yemaya, Innana, Flora, Hera , Gaia, Asherah, Esmeralda,
Freya, Mawu, Danu, Ishtar, The Corn Mothers, Vesta, and Rhea.

HERSTORY:

The European Wicce Goddess of Midsummer is Cerridwen. She is abundance, fertility and power, and Midsummer becomes a celebration of these desirable qualities.

"Pele, the great Goddess of the fire of Hawaii's volcanos, lives in the South. Her hair and breath are the flowing rivers of lava which erupt with sudden and devastating power. She represents the absolute supremacy of Nature over the thoughts and plans of humanity. Once the will has been aligned and personal expression discovered, South becomes the direction of love and the healing energy that can flow through the heart and hands. This is the fire of the heart that heals, the green fields and warm rocks of summer."[10]

The Earth is midpoint on her journey around the Sun. It is the first day of summer and the longest and strongest day of the year. The Sun, at her peak of power, rises and sets as far to the South as she gets, making her highest arc in the sky. It is the last outbreath of the Earth, who is strong, outgoing, primal energy, and in her time everything grows. From this point on, daylight begins to decrease and the nights lengthen.

Midsummer celebrates the full powers of life and the beginning of the change from a waxing to a waning year. We look forward to the inward-looking peace of the dark. Midsummer is a celebration of the South, fire, and summer. In Brazil this is a Festival of the Sea as the Goddess Iamanja is honored. Priestesses keep a perpetual fire burning at her shrine, and She is worshipped with small boats covered with flowers which are set out to the ocean.

In Europe, Midsummer was a three-day festival of dancing, lovemaking and raucous behavior. There were bonfires to celebrate the Sun and the people jumped the flames, making wishes. There was an "old wives tale" that the summer grains would grow only as high as they were able to jump, so this became an athletic event to benefit the community.

"Summer Solstice is the Festival of the Goddesses of the South Corner, of creative energy, of the Corn Mothers of Native Americans, the Phoenix of Old Egypt, and of bonfires and fire-leaping Goddesses. When outdoor fire-leaping rituals attract too much attention, there are simple alternatives. A wok might be filled with sand and votive candles and set on a nest of green branches or driftwood in the center of your circle. Or use a handmade broom, the Wand, transformed by our wary foremothers of the Burning Times to conceal and protect, the ancient symbol of spiritual authority as rooted in fire energy. The broom may be placed so the womyn leap or dance over it.

"Since all life is a cycling of endings and beginnings, go first for purification. Cleanse the old by passing through the ring of fire, as through confrontation and anger, and go out the other side to something bright and smooth and cool, like action. Leap again and again, to forge courage, strength, and resilience! Become a labyris, the tool of gathering and self-defense, ready to harm none and do your will! Remember, that in all fire there is the ash of earth; in all action there is stillness, and in summer there is winter (and summer again)."[11] We are in full bloom, abundant and energetic. Our creativity flows.

"Traditionally, European witches go into the forest and gather herbs to produce more concentrated oils for the festival. Covens sometimes make garlands of mugwort, vervain and St. Joan's Wort to wear as adornments during the festival. Pumpernickel bread, symbolizing the dark, rich earth, is passed around, being consumed with as much fervor as the work of making magic.

"Tribes come together to travel to old homesteads to visit with family and friends. Spells include blessings on future tasks, love, weather, protection, and general celebrations of wimmin.

"For protection in the coming year, jump over a balefire or candle. If there is a pressing issue at hand, write it in red ink on white paper, smear the paper with honey, fold gently and burn it saying, 'I give my sorrow to the flames, the Goddess of Fire will consume my pain. It is done.'

"It is said if a person stares at Midsummer's fires through bunches of larkspur that his or her sight will be strengthened. Scrying, fortune telling, and other forms of divination (often affairs of the heart) are practiced.

"This is also the season when fairies and spirits of the forest are abroad and revelling. Offerings of wild thyme should be made to these shy creatures. If the Sabbat is performed outside, ring the circle with wild thyme and mark the quarters with wild heather as these are most pleasing to the deities at this time. The incense that you use might be pine or wisteria."[12]

The Altar:

Using a wheel-shaped base, we weave a solstice wheel from the greenery, flowers and herbs we have gathered. The flower wheel is used as an altar piece which also symbolizes the fullness of the green earth in this season. Roses, especially, are flowers of Midsummer. If they are available, crowns of roses are made for all wimmin to wear.

All flowers, red especially (the color of passion), adorn the altar, which is also covered with a red cloth. Red candles, the fruits of summer, and symbols of abundance and love, such as heart shapes, are part of the Solstice Altar. Midsummer is sacred to the Fire Queen of Love.

Suggested Ritual:

This is the warmest time of the year. Outdoor rituals are possible now when everything is in full bloom. If there is no danger of fire, a bonfire can be set earlier in the day for the evening's festivities.

As many of us who can meet early in the afternoon to gather flowers, berries, and herbs for the ritual and for adorning our naked bodies. We laugh and play in the woods, swim in the creek, ocean, or stream.

Games of strength are organized and played: races, wrestling, athletic events. Drumming is an important feature of this play day. If there are experienced drummers in your group, ask them to bring their congas for the afternoon and the evening ritual. Drumming, dancing, and singing are good ways to raise energy and the cone of power, and summer solstice is the most energetic day of the year.

To invoke memories of Amazon times, the circle is cast by two athletic wimmin running the boundaries three times, shoulders and arms linked. They can do this in silence or accompanied by chanting from the other wimmin.

The directions are addressed, the wimmin are smudged.

Priestess:

"Today we celebrate our strengths and power as womyn. The flames of the candles and fire represent our energy and passion. With our dances and our songs we celebrate life to its fullest."

The Bonfire and candles are lit.

A candle is passed around, to the left, and each womon repeats:

"My name is Ffiona, I am a powerful womon." She then states the ways in which she is powerful in her life. The group repeats, "As we say it, so shall it be," after each womon has spoken.

The rattle is passed several times. When you have the rattle, you can ask the group to focus on your wishes or share a poem, dance, story, or song. Wimmin jump the bonfire, as high as they are able, making wishes as they do. Also, herbs and slips of paper with lists of those things in your life, your character, your environment, that you wish to be rid of, are thrown into the flames accompanying wishes.

Love spells are cast on this night. Everyone wishing a love spell can bring to the group an idea of exactly how she wishes it done. Z. Budapest's *Grandmother of Time* has a couple of very potent Love spells, or you can compose your own.

A vulva-shaped bowl, shell, or conch is passed around the circle, full of honey, along with a smaller bowl of cut persimmons, grapes, cut kiwis and other sweet fruit. As it is passed (to the left), everyone takes time to focus and put her personal power or essence into the contents. The bowl is passed a second time and wimmin dip their fingers in the honey and eat the fruit, repeating, "I taste the sweetness of life and of womyn."

The ritual is closed with drumming, the feast is prepared and the party continues.

Invocation to Summer:

"Blessed Queen of Summer, Fire Goddesses of Love and Abundance, Goddesses of The Ocean, we feel your passion stir in us today as we celebrate the fulfillment and fullness of life. Bless us, Mother of the Universe, you who are mature in your abundance.

Today we celebrate the rebirth of the darkness, gifting us with longer nights and shorter days. Guide and bless us, as we begin our journey towards the womb of Samhain."

MIDSUMMER STORY—MY YEMAYA [13]

It was a cold and rainy day for summer on the ocean. Now that I was living on this windy coast I was building woodfires in July and driving through fog so thick it was like wading through pea soup.

My bed was warm, too warm to leave. I snuggled back into the flannel sheets and contemplated my choices for the day. The ocean was pulling at me like a magnet as I listened to the sound of the surf beating on the beach outside my window.

Because of my dedication to The Earth I had decided to spend Earth Day, which was today, picking up garbage on the beach. My resolution was slipping as I considered the pouring rain and chilly fog of the shoreline. Even so, the salty smell of the sea was tantalizing to my nostrils: Yemaya called. I thought it was an act of valor to even get out of bed on a day like this..

I was in love with Yemaya, the Ocean Mother. I couldn't get enough of Her: I had dedicated myself in a ceremony on the beach just recently, after She had spoken to me and taken me to Her bosom as a daughter. It was a turning point in my life to be so committed to The Earth. I got out of bed, groaning as my feet hit the cold floor. I should get the purple heart for this one.

The beach was wet and as I walked along the shore I found profuse amounts of garbage which people had strewn on Her body. I picked it up, as in a meditation, piece by piece, methodically, Virgo-like, and put it in my bag. With each piece, I blessed the Ocean.

The rain was soaking me, but that wasn't the only reason I was upset; the amount of garbage was incredible! I couldn't believe that people would trash the beaches like this. It made me very sad and angry. I was so overwrought that I started crying and couldn't stop. The tears kept flowing, now mixing with the rain and ocean spray.

All the loneliness of the past year flooded over me, along with the frustration of facing this ravage of the environment. I'd expected this to be a day that I gave to Mother Earth, trying to do my small bit to make this world cleaner; but now it had also become a day of grieving for Her. The effect it had on me was powerful and surprisingly emotional. I had always viewed environmental issues in a detached, logical, and political way. Now I was touched to the depths of my soul.

I sobbed out my grief and isolation, When I was through She was still there, beautiful and comforting. I asked Her, "Yemaya, I love you so much, and I am so lonely, please manifest yourself in human form? All was quiet. Then I heard a voice speaking my name. "Just you, one small person *can* make a difference: tell them to stop polluting my waters. Help stop the oil tankers that are dumping their loads into my body. Tell them to make it a priority. Since you love me so much, and are so committed to the planet, I will appear to you as a womon. Your wish will be granted."

I met Lani shortly thereafter. I knew from the very beginning that she was Yemaya from the way she knew all about me without knowing me. I didn't believe in love at first sight, but I knew I loved her the moment we met. We had a month of euphoria, extremely concentrated passionate time. I was in bliss, counting my blessings. Then the problems began—they were very intense and seemed unsolvable. I felt crazy because I loved Lani; she was the ocean to me. I had to end the relationship and say goodbye, even though I loved her. I was so unhappy and miserable. I had to save my dignity.

I went to the ocean with my pain. I had to get back to Her to find out what went wrong. I prepared a poem for Her: "Yemaya, Ocean Mother, in the beginning You gave birth to the heavens, to all the Goddesses. Sister of the fishes, Yemaya, rock me, soothe me, Yemaya. You are the storm of my anger. Bring me home again, deep Ocean of love."[14]

Then I took off my clothes and jumped into the cold, pounding surf. The salt water bit into my skin, but I was exhilarated by the magic of the moment. I couldn't stay in the freezing water very long and I quickly ran from the waves to the shore, falling face-down on the sand. Miraculously, it had stopped raining and the sun had appeared from between the grey clouds. I thanked the Sun for her warmth as I lay there for a while and cried. Then I got up, put on my clothes, and walked further down the beach, immersed in my grief and depression. Lani and I had such an intense connection, drawn together by Aphrodite, Goddess of Love and Yemaya, Goddess of the Ocean. We were so close, so loving, before the trouble began. I had lost myself to her, given up parts of me that were important, sacrificed my dignity. It didn't work to do that, to abandon my own wants and needs in order to fill hers. It was too painful to be with her, yet it hurt to be away from her. The pain of lost love pierced my heart.

Lani's love was such a wonderful gift—something that might happen only once. I grieved for her, turning to face the ocean, crying to Yemaya in my pain and sorrow. "Why, Mother, did you give me the gift of this beautiful love, and then take it away?" I sat in silence thinking there would be no answer. Yet after moments of stillness I heard her voice as clear as a bell, as strong as the tide. She said, "I don't give gifts, I give lessons. And the lesson is the gift."

I was in shock at hearing Her again: this was the third time. I sat on the beach, thinking about what She'd said and waiting for more messages. They didn't come. It was getting late, so I went home.

When I arrived at my house, the answering machine had a message from Lani saying, "Why don't you give me a call. I really want to see you—I want you in my life—I miss you." I thought of my obsessive behavior, how I had acted before, and I knew it would be a while before I could embrace my Yemaya again. I needed time to look deeply into myself and learn my lessons.

The biggest lesson Yemaya gave me was to look at my obsessive behavior and see how I lost my personal power when I loved someone. Revelations like that don't always seem healing at the time and aren't necessarily fun, but I know they are necessary for my growth and I have learned to appreciate what I receive from them.

I think that those of us on the Goddess Path seem to be given more than our share of these hard lessons. Of course, there's always the highs of talking to the ocean to balance things out.

LAMMAS (LOAF MASS)—FESTIVAL OF THE BREAD
July 31 - August 2
Direction: West

So we go a year around
The wheel that everturning
Brings the circle into spiral
Out to circle, spinning, yearning

Follow moons and quarters, sabbats
Follow harvest, darkness, death
Follow spring to life and ripening
Follow spirals, no regrets

Each in season turns the wheel
Each the spiral dance must dream
Each in wider circles, spinning
Finds the pattern in the scheme
                                        Ila Suzanne

Theme:

First Fruits

Goddesses:

Habondia, The Corn Mothers, Fortuna, Prosperina

HERSTORY:

Lammas, also called Lady Day, is the third cross-quarter fire festival and the high point between Summer Solstice and Fall Equinox. Now the Sun is over its yearly peak and slowly begins to lose power as the days become visibly shorter. It is still hot summer, but she is nearing her end. We celebrate the darkness returning.

Lammas is a celebration of the first fruits of the harvest season presided over by Habondia, Goddess of Abundance. She then becomes The Reaper of the Harvest.

To Native Americans this is the season of the Sundance and Green Corn Ceremony. To Pagans, Lammas honors the mystery of the growing grain which transforms herself into the life-giving element of bread. As witches we celebrate this first harvest to give thanks to Mother Earth for sharing Her gifts. Our foremothers took their first fruits as offerings to the temples of the Goddess.

"During ancient Pagan times the tribes would have fairs and markets in which to sell their wares, show and race their horses and hold conferences. Some climbed holy mountains and performed a ritual, sacrificing something valuable to them, so the Earth would be fertile and bear fruit for the coming year........Fertility rites and rituals for material abundance were held".[15]

The Altar

The altar is again draped in red or gold, symbolizing summer's heat, fire, and the Mother aspect of The Goddess. On the altar are placed seeds and first fruits of the garden and fields: cobs of corn, cornmeal, grapes, barley cakes, loaves of bread of all kinds (preferably handmade by wimmin) and corn or bread figures shaped like womyn. Vegetables of all kinds from the gardens are brought and corn dolls made of dried corn husks are placed in the east, west, north and south parameters of the circle. After the ritual these corn dolls are kept in a special place until next Lammas.

Apples for Diana and garlic for Hecate are also included as Lammas is near their celebration on August 13th. Z. Budapest tells us, "While Diana/Artemis was the soul of nature who protected the living and the young, Hecate also protected the dead souls, or those who were about to enter the realms of the dead. She was worshipped at the crossroads."[16] Hecate, Lady of the Gates guides the soul from this life into the next. We honor these Goddesses by blessing the animals.

As some groups do on all eight holydays, we gather to dance the spiral and turn the wheel. On Lammas, day of fullness, there is an opening and renewing of heart energy between sisters. We realize we have received so much more than we asked the Goddess for that we share it with those we love. The energy we have put into our gardens and fields is beginning to return to us in food, as well as love. We have worked together with the earth to produce the fruit, grain, and vegetables and we are humbled by the abundance: our labors have been rewarded. Today we also focus on Fortuna, Goddess of Good Fortune. It's a good time to cast spells for love, health, and money.

"Thank you for the potato,
Thank you.....thank you......for the potato..
Gift from the earth,
The earth giving me, Energy
For life, for life,
For life...........for life."

By Peepa Pinon

And when Lammas is over, we turn inward in preparation for the harvest of Fall Equinox.

Suggested Ritual:

Wimmin gather to celebrate Lammas on the night before to sleep in a dream wheel formation. This means that a circle is formed, heads in the center, and bodies fanning out like spokes in a wheel. Wimmin's feet form the outside parameter of the circle. A fire in the center is optional. If the dreamwheel is done on Lammas eve, keep the ritual fire burning all night. On Lammas morning dreams are shared with the group. The circle is cast with seeds to mark the boundaries.

Invocation:

"Blessed Habondia, Goddess of Plenty, Baker of the Bread of Life, teach us how to plant our seeds and manifest the abundance we deserve: abundance of the mind and creativity, abundance of the heart, the material realm, and of energy.

"Fortuna, Goddess of Good Fortune, show us how to make our lives a living example of prosperity in all ways. Show us how to trust that our sharing and giving will return to us, over and over. May we be ever grateful for these gifts from your sacred body.

"Diana/Artemis, Goddess of the Living, Lady of the Beasts, we are thankful for your gifts of the four-leggeds, animal companions who walk with us. Bless them, these our friends, and heal those animals who are endangered species, and those who have lost their homes to the two-leggeds. Make a place for them, always."

The Priestess offers a libation to the Harvest. A chalice is passed around and each woman gives a toast to her personal prosperity and harvest.

Drumming begins and the spiral is formed, the turning of the wheel begins. As we dance the spiral we sing, "Happiness, health, and prosperity, for everyone." (over and over).

We also sing the song of thanks, "We want to thank you Goddess, thank you Goddess, thank you Goddess, thank you. Thank you for the things that you do. We want to thank you Goddess......etc. Thank you for loving us too."

When the spiral is done, the Cone of Power is formed by chanting the names of Lammas Goddesses or the "Ma" chant.

This is a time to share our abundance so several passes of the rattle are made around the circle. A basket containing the bread-womon figures is also passed, each womon taking two. The Priestess asks the circle to psychically put anything we want to release into one of the figures (for example, our sorrows, fears, pain). The figures are then thrown into the fire, each womon declaring (if she wishes), "I give my sorrow (pain, etc.) to the flames."

We feed the second figure to the sister on our left, repeating the words, "Eat the bread of life, may you never hunger." The conch shell is passed, full of fresh spring water, "May you always have an abundance of sweet liquid to quench your thirst."

Before the ritual everyone has made necklaces and bracelets of seeds strung on thread and these are now exchanged. Acacia flowers are burned for those hoping to find love.

Photographs of animal companions are passed around and each womon shares stories about her animal friend.   Songs of abundance are sung and the bonfire is kept burning. The womyn are satiated. All is well. The circle is closed.

Priestess:

"We journey inward this night to a place of waiting, a place of change. We are grateful for these first fruits and the abundant harvest that is still to come."

The directions are thanked. Feasting begins.

A dream circle can be formed around the fire.

LAMMAS STORY—BREAD BABIES

(This is not a true story. It was inspired by *'A Lesbian Appetite,'* by D. Allison, from her fantastic book, *Trash*).

You are called The Goddess Diana in Rome, The Goddess Artemis in Greece. I call you lover. Your name has the ring of a silver bell, or the clear tone of a crystal bowl. Your celebration is close to Lammas, just after first fruits, time of Habondia, Goddess of Abundance. First harvest is here and the bread is baked.....bread, oh yes, the bread!

We are the daughters of Diana. For me you are the first fruits of a barren and dry summer. The day we met it rained— refreshingly clear, light, falling rain. I looked into your eyes and was carried back in time, far into the past, long ago when we were together in Wales, somewhere on the cliffs of that Celtic coast. In you I saw myself. Abundance, you are abundance sinking into my abundance. I am your daily bread. I dive into your waters.

I was parched from the summer's heat and the loss of my longest and dearest love. I called on Aphrodite and she gave me you....wild, bold, uncontrollable you. Goddess of life: Diana/Artemis, all the animals come when you speak.

We make the bread—an ancient womoon's art. Lammas (loaf-mass) bread, from the first fruits of the grown grain. Together we grind wheat in the hand-grinder; hours of labor, our sweating bodies drip in the August heat. The dough rises and our passion rises with the bread. I reach under the cloth covering the dough and grab a handful, then playfully shove it between your breasts which blossom up from your thin summer shirt. You retaliate by also grabbing a handful, pulling up my blouse, and smearing the sticky mess over my stomach, pretending to knead bread. I kiss you hard and long. You knead me, now, pushing your face into my stomach, then between my legs. Giggling, we both fall to the floor, hands still dusty with flour, gobs of sticky dough between us. I reach between your legs, planting another handful there— your juices run into the bread dough.   "Put me in your oven and bake me", you say.

First fruits. Ripe, shiny apples, ruby red tomatoes, deep purple eggplants, and fresh green zucchini. First corn, white and yellow juicy kernels in pale green leaves. First grains; rye, wheat, oats. To make the bread.

You make me giggle, then gasp, as you munch on my vulva, eating my fresh fruits. I lick the bread dough off your persimmon and my tongue searches for your kiwi. I plant another handful of bread on your thighs. Your juices flow and flow, into the dough. We grab more and more of it, smearing it on our bodies as our clothes are removed, piece by piece. The kitchen heat rises and summer clothes peel off easily. I lay you out on the kitchen rug, and we kiss and kiss and kiss, tasting the fruits of our ripe lips, strawberry pink and cherry red. Laughing and rolling on the floor, food everywhere, we make sacred love, mixing the bread dough with our juices. Abundant first fruits of summer. This is my summer. You joke with me when we're not laughing or kissing or loving, "We must knead the dough, knead the dough ."

After we're done we salvage what we can of the bread dough, knead it for awhile, then put it to rest under the cool cloth. Then we go down to the river and each washes off all the dried and sticky dough from the other's body, gently caressing as we do. We make love again, this time on the sandy beach.

As we eat the bread later, we smile into each other's eyes, remembering its preparation. You offer a piece to your mother, I offer one to my friend..... Abundance......We smile.

FALL EQUINOX—MABON,
Equal Night and Equal Day—September 19-23
Direction - West

The harvest is in
Food stored for the winter
Seeds secreted for spring
Celebrate the inward journey
Join Persephone as she descends
Motherearth turns toward crone
As we dance the last dance
Half is day, half is night
Harvest moon, orange sight
Bless the dance, bless the rite
Half is day, half is night
Half is dark, half is light
Spiral out, spiral in
Harvest, death, rebirth again
Goddesselves blessing all wimmin
Who spiral out and spiral in
                                    Ila Suzanne

Theme:

Giving Thanks—The Harvest—Balance

Goddesses:

Mama Cocha, Incan Goddess of the Harvest;
Bethulta, Hebrew Goddess of Virgo, who is Abundance of
the Harvest; Ceres and Demeter.

HERSTORY:

Mabon—early Thanksgiving harvest dinner—weather magic
for rain. The sun's path crosses over the equator, travelling
South. We celebrate the lengthening darkness as the whole world
honors equal night and day. Summer is gone. We gather the fruits
and vegetables from our garden, and give away what we don't
need. It is when we reap what we have sown at Spring Equinox.
Food is stored and prepared for winter. The fall air is brisk and
duller colors appear. Everything turns with the season, the
leaves blow in the wind. We can still feel the waning presence
of the sun. There is a restlessness in the air, the mood is solemn.
The Harvest Moon is round and wheat colored, glowing from the
sun, like our brown and black summer bodies.

As we see the flaming colors of the leaves, we remember that
life burns most intensely just before it dies. We remember those
friends who have died in the past year as we watch the falling of
the leaves.

Autumn Equinox is a Harvest Celebration honoring Demeter,
Queen of the Harvest. It is also the witches' thanksgiving after
the harvest has been gathered. We give thanks for this
abundance. This is the beginning of the season of death. The sun
is about to enter Libra, cardinal air sign of balance. Persephone
goes underground until the spring.

**Moving to the soft darkness which beckons
and draws us in again.
Towards the part that lives in shadow -- out of focus
Moving from logic to intuition
Activity is suspended and the veil between the worlds is thin.**

"Autumn equinox is the witches' thanksgiving; it is the time
of Kore's descent, Lucina's farewell, and the Skirophoria, the
descent of the virgins to Aphrodite's sanctuary. In Mesopotamia,
vulvas of lapis lazuli are presented to Ishtar. Autumn is the time
of Indian wimmin's ceremonies. Iroquois wimmin do dances of
"what we live on"—the wimmin's shuffle dance, the corn dance,
the squash dance. They sing harvest songs, songs which are
individually created and owned. Hopi wimmin separate for Lakon,
the corn harvest ceremony, playing and singing in the kiva
(underground holy site) and spending all night on the mesa. As
the melons mature, they observe Marawa, a time of wommon's
sexuality and power demonstrated by leg markings symbolic of

their menstrual periods. When the melons are drying on the vine, wimmin participate in the basket dance. All are celebrations of wommon's control of the food supply and fertility."[17]

Autumn Equinox is a time of balance and equilibrium, of repose and resting after the labors of planting and harvesting. It is when we give thanks, gather and store. We compost and mulch our gardens, returning to the earth in thankfulness what She has given us; we recycle and review, enjoy the fruits of our labors, appreciating a time of plenty in preparation for a time of scarcity. This is a day and night of feasting: the Harvest meal is prepared. We share our plenty with those who do not have enough.

"This season, more than others, signifies the movement of time through nature, the drastic changes in color and the obvious shortening of the days. We feel the gentle stirrings toward "nest-feathering" and preparing for the coming winter. It's also a season of "accounting", taking stock of our "harvest", reviewing and evaluating where we stand, and knowing our strengths and our weaknesses."[18]

"Fall Equinox is the High point of the harvest. It is the time to stand back from your work and take stock of the year's achievements, to thank the Corn Mother, Demeter, the Goddess of Grain, and to congratulate each other. Of course it is also time to evaluate our political situation as wimmin on the national and international scene. Matriarchal traditions lingering in Ancient Greece provided a separate holiday Thesmophoria Oct. 11-13, (Holy Book of Women's Mysteries Part 1 p. 110-112) for the official gathering of women to list and settle injustices and offenses. Within the comprehensive political and social scope of the festival was included a bitching session in which personal conflicts were aired and even squared with a bit of ritualized rough-housing.

"Since most of us are not directly involved in the harvesting of precious grain, and its compliment of ergot, the Equinox is a good time to balance the scales and even some scores through a grievance process and a political spell or two, and, for the committed, a dramatic public event. Certainly we are all vulnerable through the ecological network and need to protect the food producing lands through the political process by raising consciousness around our fragile matrix, our Mother, the Earth.

"Autumn is the season of consciousness governed by air energy and the expansive communicating mind. It follows summer's watery pleasures and intuitions, the spring's fire and renewal. Remember the autumn air by adding freshly gathered herbs and seeds to mojo bags and medicine supplies. Sprinkle some on the incense cauldron and return some to the earth. Be joyful and generous in praising and righteous in cursing, for this is Persephone's fulfillment in the season of heightened consciousness."[19]

This is the season of giving, of changing, and introspection. We look into ourselves and assess who we are and where we're going. We prepare for the physical and spiritual survival of winter.

Fall is the time of turning leaves and turning inward. A point of balance. Balancing out all the internal debris; keeping some, letting some go. It is when we balance out relationships and energy commitments. Now we examine our reasons for practicing the Craft and rededication to it. Initiations can be performed now. We embrace the richness, and in it, find our own inner darkness.

Celtic symbols of Mabon are the whistling swan and titmouse bird. The month is dedicated to poetry and poets. The entire world celebrates equal day and night as the sun passes over the equator travelling south.

The Altar:

Fall, sunset colors, fall browns, greens, deep reds and burnt oranges, deep gold. The color of the Fall Equinox is red rust.

Wimmin gather in twilight. Food: breads, hot dishes, cider juice, pumpkins, squashes, gourds, apples and corn are on the altar. The green altar cloth is decorated with leaves, candles, wreaths, pine cones, oak leaves, acorns and nuts.

Brooms are placed on the altar to sweep away our internal debris. (Smaller ones can be used to brush auras for purification.)

Suggested Ritual for Fall Equinox:

An unlit Fire is set, outdoors if possible. The circle is cast, directions are addressed, with special attention given to the West.

Priestess: " Tonight we move from the high energy of summer to the peace of winter in the balance of equal day and night. Blessed be the day, for in the day we see clearly what we must change." She lights yellow candles.

"Blessed be the night, for in the night we confront ourselves in all our beauty and imperfections." She lights dark blue candles, and chants:

> **"Earth my body, Water my blood,
> Air my breath, and Fire my spirit."**

Light the bonfire or cauldron.

Priestess: "Let us remember those we love who have died, whose memories are ever with us. We join hands and remember those special ones who have died since the last autumn equinox:"

Fall Equinox Chant:

**Equal dark and equal light, All love is equal in Her sight
Equal dark and equal light, All are equal in Her sight**[20]

(The following can be part of this Ritual or a separate one):

"Bitching Session"

Priestess: "Tonight we acknowledge our faults and weaknesses and ask for forgiveness. We relinquish all grudges, forgiving others."

Go around the circle to the left, passing the rattle. Each womon speaks of her held resentments. Apple juice is shared for libations. Some is poured out on the ground by the Priestess.

Priestess: "We remember the sweetness of life as we taste the sweetness of this juice."

The ritual is closed.

Invocation to Fall Equinox:

Demeter, Giver of Life and Plenty, you ripened the grain, the fruits, the nuts of the earth. Thank you for the fullness of this season. We say goodbye to the bright days of summer and begin to celebrate the coming darkness. May we always live in hope.

MABON STORY—FANNY'S LAUGHTER[21]

The time had come. I could see that when I entered the room and found her. I suddenly realized there would be a half an hour, at the most, to do what I had promised before she died.

Oh, Fanny! I have tended your body and loved your kind heart and great spirit for these last three years. Now you've picked your time to leave the planet, and I don't quite know if I'm ready to say goodbye with such short notice.

Enough! I must hurry! I start moving through the small, old-fashioned house, gathering all the things I need to prepare Fanny for her big transition. Let me see...soap, water, comb, clothes, towels, bedsheets. My heart is thumping like a jackhammer; this is my first human death. I've seen the animals take their leave, in fact, helped some of them pass on. But, one of my human kin......I'm scared, just as scared as the time Ma took on the rattlesnake. That was a life-and-death situation too, down by the creek beside the house. That huge coiled snake just sittin' there clicking away with its rattlers...clickety-click, at the cat who was going into trance (we could see that), blissed out, not moving a *muscle*. Ma did a fine thing then, making all that noise and yelling for us kids to come, all seven of us, to go get the pots and pans from the house. There we were, every last one of us, clanging and banging on those pots and yelling at that snake to leave. It was the stick that finally saved the cat, that long curved stick that Mavis shoved her out of the way with. We all kept up the racket, a'yellin' and a'screamin' like banshees. I must admit I started talking in my head to that snake so she'd leave, asking her to co-operate, and fast, so Ma wouldn't have to use the shotgun on her. I kept concentrating real hard on that request. Meanwhile everyone kept up the racket. I do that a lot, you know, talk to the animals in my head. If my friends or family knew, they'd think I was stir-crazy. But you know, the animals seem to listen and understand me, even though no words are spoken.

Well, all of a sudden, to the amazement of us all, that snake took one last look at our crazy bunch and just slithered away. Yes, ma'am, just slithered away!! And we never saw her again. Ma said she was only lookin' for water, and that was a good lesson in learnin' there are more ways to deal with the creatures than running for the shotgun.

Why am I thinking of that!! Fanny needs me!! Now...I'm finally through speeding around, out of breath from carrying this big mound of clothes and wash-up supplies to her room. I keep asking the Goddess of Death to appear on the scene and sort of direct things for us, due to my lack of knowledge in such matters.

The room is dark. I turn up the blinds and open the window. Sweet sunlight and fresh air pour in. "Smell that, Fanny! Just breathe in the fragrance from those lilacs you planted outside the window."

Fanny doesn't answer, and I wonder if it's already too late, until I notice her breathing. I begin moving with a great energy that seems to be propelling me from Fanny's spirit as she lays there, eyes shut, but fluttering now and then, lettin' me know she's hanging in there till everything is done just how she wants it, just how I've promised. Bed changed....clean...Fanny washed...clean, with her favorite Yardley cologne driftin' from her, reminding me of smells and sounds of the past, of a different way of life we no longer know. She wears her new peach lace dress, the soft, silky, one that makes you want a dish of orange sherbet every time you look at it. I gently comb her thick white hair, still beautiful, even in Death. Ever since she was a girl, she has had that beautiful hair, kept it natural too. The beauty of this spunky old woman radiated in these, her last hours.

At peace, finally, I sit beside her bed, her hand in mine. I know I finished just in time. She is silent and her breath is becoming more and more shallow. "I did everything you wanted me to do, Fanny," I abruptly say. She doesn't answer me. Her form is silent, but I can still feel her spirit. A hummingbird flies around the open window, gathering pollen from Fanny's lilacs.

Suddenly, she half-rises in bed, opens her eyes, and lets out a laugh. It is such a fine, loud laugh, "Ah, ha, ha", and then falls back on the pillows, a smile on her face. She closes her eyes. I know she is gone.

A laugh! What a great gift, that laugh, as if to say, "It's so easy, so easy this dyin'. Why didn't ya tell me it was so easy? I'd have done it sooner!" Now I sit in the quiet aftermath of her wonderful death and give thanks for the gift of Fanny's laughter. I look over at her body and I can see a shimmer of translucent lights, a misty shape rising, sinuously, like the snake. It is the snake, and I immediately know that here is my Goddess of Death, my symbol of transformation and rebirth. I say goodbye to Fanny as I leave the room, saying "Goodbye Fanny, see you later, over a cup of tea and a good laugh!"

Let us die living
Let us live our dying.

SAMHAIN ("Sow-win"), ALL HALLOWS EVE, HALLOMAS[22]
WITCHES' NEW YEAR—October 31
Direction: North

Time of Hag Time of Crone
Time of Blood, Time of Bone
Hecate offers cold embrace
Spectre, wraith and banshee pace
Wait for Hallow's eve to fly
Wait 'til deepest dark to scry
This night the veil is very thin
Life goes out and death comes in
Open wide to all the fear
Trust that from the darkness here
Life and light will rise again
Death goes out and life comes in
                                        Ila Suzanne

Theme:

Death and Rebirth

Goddesses of All Hallows:

Hecate—Dark Goddess of the Crossroads, of Death and Rebirth,
who will one day greet us all;
Kali Ma—The Destroyer and Awakener, She who destroys
only what is needed to further growth;
Baba Yaga—Russian Crone Goddess of Death, the Sacred Hag;
Kalma, Mari, Sina, Hela, Sarama, Sedna, Skinmo, Seshat and Hathor

HERSTORY:

Samhain is the celebration of Hags and Crones, who bring the wisdom of the ages as well as death, destruction and renewal. The Crone of Samhain is the Third Aspect of the Goddess as Avenger, Destroyer, and Protector of Womyn.

Witches fly high on Samhain, or All Hallows Eve, the fourth Wiccan fire festival, where all crossroads come together. The old year dies and the new begins; a time of purification and renewal. We honor the dark, as the days get shorter and the nights get longer. At Samhain, the veils are the thinnest between the worlds, and now we can most easily make a bridge to the spirit world to contact our ancestors and friends who are dead. We bring them to life: they visit us by a warm bonfire.

This is also the time for remembering the 13 million (plus) witches who were tortured, burned, drowned, stoned, and hung during the Inquisition and at Salem, Massachusetts.

We witness the Goddess transformed from the fresh young Maiden of Spring, innocent and childlike, to the Mother of Summer, and now to a beloved and wise old Crone. It is a time of transition and change, from autumn to winter, and a time when we deliberately change reality with dress and costumes in order to fool ourselves and each other. At Samhain there is potent fixed energy, the power to draw in life to our own magnetic center.

"The mask has always been one of our most magnetically powerful bewitching tools. Behind the mask, each woman's power to attract and magnetize is enhanced a thousandfold. It is also the mask which serves as a shield to maintain a distance. The illusion behind the mask then becomes an object of great desire, a treasure to be discovered."[23]

Animals speak to us on Samhain. We create illusions with costumes and impersonate animals, who are invoked for our protection and power. Now we have power over all the evil oppression around us. It is a time for scrying, working with trance states, prophecies, automatic writing, and crystal ball gazing. Messages from the other-world reach out and touch us, gifting us with the realization that this is not the only world or the only life. A new flame is kindled as bonfires blaze on the hilltops. Often, the Spiral Dance is performed symbolizing the movement from death to rebirth.

The Altar:

Samhain honors the dark, the Crone, and the underworld. The altar is hung with veils. Use red and black candles to symbolize life and death. It is also an ancestor altar, with symbols, photos, writings, and prayers to our ancestors: places are set at the feasting table for them. Fall dying leaves decorate the altar to the dead.

Apples and pomegrametes, fruits that symbolize death and rebirth, (the pomegranate of Icore, the fruit of life) are placed on the altar. Red food and drink is brought and consumed. The yeast Bread of the Dead, baked with newly harvested grain, loaves with arms, legs, and faces sprinkled with sesame seeds, adorn the altar. The pumpkin of plenty abounds. If the ritual is done inside, boughs of greens are laid.

Suggested Ritual:

The circle is opened, Directions are cast. Large bunches of flowers are brought in remembrance for all the witches who died in the Patriarchal Holocaust (The Inquisition).

As we enter the circle, red moons are painted on each womon's forehead. Wimmin come dressed/masked, prepared to sit around the bonfire all night (to be adapted for those who are unable).

As the circle is being cast to the left (doesil), The Priestess walks (on the outside) to the right (widdershins) and chants:

"We all come from the Darkness, and to Her we shall return. Darkness, darkness, be our teacher, fill us with your velvet night, gathering power. Know that there is great comfort in sleep and the dark hours of night. Tonight we journey there, then rebirth ourselves again."

The ritual fire is lit (a bonfire, if outdoors). Wimmin have brought candles carved with names, which are placed in front of them. The circle is opened by the following call to the dead.

Priestess:

"You, who have passed to another plane—ancestors, daughters, mothers, grandmothers, lovers, we remember you. Sister witches who have suffered great oppression and death at the hands of evil, we remember you. Sisters who have died in the flames that seared your flesh; sisters gagged who have drowned in the water, or under the piles of stones crushing you forever. We remember you.

"May your raging, howling, crying spirits know peace and join us tonight as we honor you who have gone before us, who have paved the way and created our few freedoms with your deaths. We bless you, witch ancestors. Join us in our New Year celebration.

Samhain Chant:

Everything that dies is reborn.
Everything that dies is reborn.
· There is no end. There is no end.
(Repeat and repeat)

The black Samhain Candles are lit.

The Priestess chants, "We invite you in— spirits of the dead, spirits of our ancestors".

The rattle is passed around the circle, to the left, and each womon speaks, sings, or calls to the ancestor(s) she invites to the circle. The Cone of power is raised and sent to heal all witches of oppression and to protect us from evil.

After this is done, drumming, masks, and additional costumes are donned. Dancing and singing are done with our ancestors. The veils that are hanging from the altar are removed.

Chant names of Crone and Hag Goddesses on this night.

Womon dressed as Kali chants:

"I am Kali—the outraged avenger of all wimmin. I awaken you to your incredible dark power. I shred the veils of illusion and destroy that which holds you back from growth. Honor Me."

Womon dressed as Hecate: (dark robes, old womon mask)

"I am Hecate. I stand at the crossroads of the old and new, life and death. Like the scorpion that stings, I teach you how to defend yourselves with your magic and remove those who block your path. I am the radical feminist, avenger of wimmin. Honor Me. Protect all wimmin in danger, those in bondage to men, those in prison, those sick and destitute."

All wimmin chant "Kali" and "Hecate".

Priestess: "The Goddess as Avenger and Destroyer is our guide tonight. Samhain brings us power over the male principle. It is the time we jump the bonfire repeating names of men we wish removed from our path, who have inflicted pain or evil on us or our sisters."

Wimmin jump the fire, repeating names of oppressors.

All tokens or symbols of oppression are burned in the fire, with chants, words or songs, to cast the spell. We also burn pieces of paper with qualities or outworn ways of relating that hinder our growth that we wish to banish. Repeat the spell out loud three times to banish. If done indoors, a flaming cauldron can be used.

Chant:

Blessed Be, Blessed Be,
The Transformation of Energy.
(repeat and repeat)

The rattle is passed, and the circle is closed. Those who wish can, stay the night by the fire, singing, chanting and sharing. If you wish a scrying, this is the night for it. See *Ritual For Scrying*, Chapter 3.

Invocation to The Dead:

Breaths[24]

Listen more often to things
Than to beings
'Tis the ancestors' breath
When the fire's voice is heard
'Tis the ancestors' breath
In the voice of the water

Those who have died
Have never, never left
The dead are not under the earth.
They are in the rustling trees
They are in the groaning woods
They are in the crying grass
They are in the moaning rocks
The dead are not under the earth

Those who have died
Have never, never left
The dead have a pact with the living
They are in the woman's breast
They are in the wailing child
They are with us in the home
They are with us in a crowd
The dead have a pact with the living

SAMHAIN STORY—THE CRONES OF SCORPIO

The moon was full and I had been thinking about death all day, and about Hecate. I had felt her large and intense presence before, under the chill silver-blue moon and fog of the ocean cliffs. I shivered, recalling our last encounter.

That Full Moon night I was on my way home from a friend's house. It was very late and I was nervous being out on the road alone. As I drove through the night, I slowly became aware of a large bird riding in the passenger seat, its huge, powerful wings folded, alert, and ready to pounce at the slightest disruption. I looked at it only through the corner of my eye: I was too appalled to turn my head and fully acknowledge its presence. It stared straight ahead and made no sound; its aura was menacing and foreboding. I was shocked and frozen in my seat, not knowing how I was going to drive. At that precise moment, the lights of my car went out and the darkness descended on my terrified soul. The adrenaline started racing through my body at breakneck speed. I pulled quickly off the road and jumped out. Emotionally I was panic-stricken, feeling like I was walking on the edge of a giant abyss: I decided working on my car would possibly ground me. I forced myself to lift up the creaky hood, not knowing what creature awaited me there. I was fortunate enough to find a flashlight, and I proceeded to investigate the lights, even though all I could think about was the winged one in the car. I jiggled the wires, checked the fuses and tried to strike a bargain, but she would have none of it. The car lights were a mystery to me, mazes of hoops and rubbers, but I had always been able to reason with them before. After a goodly length of time and many failures, I gave up and sat down to figure what I could do to save myself. The creature was still watching me. I was known for my Scorpio self-control, but now it had deserted me entirely: I was emotionally on the edge, and becoming very cold. I didn't want to get back into the car with Death sitting in the passenger seat.

As I considered my options a truck pulled up. I looked at the inhabitants—five men. **Five men!!!!** The reality of the situation hit me full force. All my fears that were already moving at top speed shifted into overdrive. I knew the rape statistics well and the chance of a woman alone in a deserted place with five men, escaping unharmed, was very slim. I was a sitting duck out here alone on this deserted road in the middle of the night. I immediately began appealing to the spirits because at that point I realized the situation was out of my control and my fate was surely in Her hands. I did something I'd only read about in books, I consciously turned the situation over to the Goddess. Perhaps She had a better idea on how to proceed. This act of surrender somewhat lessened my terror long enough to think logically of the next step.

They tried for quite some time to fix my car lights, and like me, did not succeed. I had regained some of my self-control, and like the snake, I was delicately tuned to sense out the truth about people and situations. I could sense the metallic taste of danger. By now I could tell they had been drinking, and this fact lessened my chances of escape. I played for time and disguised my fear and nervousness by talking—fast. I transformed myself into an entirely different persona, the most unattractive I could imagine. I instinctively knew they must not sense the depth of my sensitivity and emotions. I described my large, gun-toting family who were waiting for me at home and expected me soon. I had them believing I had lived here all my life and was well known by all the local folks: many connections, much trouble if they messed with me. I did such a good job that I started to believe it myself.

I rode in the front of the truck with two of the men, while the others rode in the back of the pickup. There was an undercurrent of expectation and tension in the air. I showed no "feminine" qualities (at least what I thought they might consider feminine), found some gum in my bag, which I chewed strenuously and loudly, and talked, and talked and talked. I wore out their ears. I turned them off—totally. By the time we were approaching my home they couldn't wait to be rid of me. As we arrived at the small cluster of cabins by the ocean I asked to be let out by the mailboxes, not wanting them to know which house was mine, just in case they changed their mind or decided they wanted to rob or rape me anyway, just for being so obnoxious.

I walked directly to a neighbor's house that I knew was deserted most of the year, and as I approached, I slid into the bushes surrounding the house and stayed there until I heard the truck drive off. I then moved quickly and stealthily to my yard and quietly crept down the cliff path to the small, hidden platform overlooking that vast and endless sea. For what seemed like an eternity, but was actually only a few minutes, I sat there trembling and shivering. The moon was glittering, bright as diamonds on the water. Then the tears came, the sobs racking my body with wave after wave of pain, releasing all the fear I had kept inside for the past few hours. I wept into the night and the sea until I felt the large dark bird who had been my companion the entire evening, fly from my side out into the ocean. I knew I had been touched by Death and Hecate and also blessed. My power of rebirth had worked another miracle and brought me home safe, though shaken.

Baba Yaga spoke to me there under the crystal-clear rays of the moon. I heard her voice in the winds: an old voice, older than the elders, older than civilization itself, older than the ancestors whose genes sing through my blood. She told me I need not be afraid, that She had been with me all through this long, hard night, and would be there again and again when I needed Her. I was stunned by Her voice; it was long and low and sang in the wind. I had heard the wind howling on the cliffs many times and it had never carried a voice before. I stayed there and listened until the singing was over and my eyelids began to droop with sleep.

I returned to my house, careful to move around without using the lights, as I knew all the other houses were dark or empty. The Goddess was doing Her part and caring for me, but I also knew I had to do my part and care for myself. This magic is a two-way agreement.

I have been through many deaths and rebirths in my time, as Scorpio always brings change as well as being a catalyst for growth in others but none of them were as profound as this.experience.

Hecate's Whereabouts

Here am I
Old Crone Hag Witchwoman of Universal knowledge!
Survivor of life's traumas Birth and Death
I am everywhere ageless
Do not turn from staring at old women
Find their courage in withered body
It is illusion that beauty sags with belly and breasts
Look again in the mirror
I am here
Ageless Crone in every generation
You find me gleefully digging for fossils and crystals
for I am durable as stone
You find me in pockmarks on the face of Sister Moon
(old scars from my childhood)
You find me in vapors belched from Mother Earth
flowing from nation to nation
across vast seas as deep
as the mysteries of my life
Crone Hag Witchwoman is you
You are Zodiac Quaballah Crystal ball
future present and past
fulfilled with wisdom of what you have accomplished
Seek me not in the physical mirrored image
for that is merely my cloak
in flux from the moment of birth
Seek me not in miasmic corruption of matter
for I am Pure Spirit within thee
You are Old Crone, Hag, and Witchwoman!

by Miriam Carroll

Notes - Chapter 4

1. Darley Adare, "The Power of Celebration," *Women of Power*, 1984, p. 77
2. Ibid.
3. Nancy F.W. Passmore, "Cyclic Time", *1978 Lunar Calendar*
4. Denise Brown and Dragon, "Wicce 101: The Wheel of the Year," *Goddess Rising*, Spring Equinox 9985.
5. Norma Joyce, *On Wings*, Vol. 5, Nos. 1 and 2, 1987, p. 5.
6. Darley Adare, *"The Power of Celebration,"* *Women of Power*, 1984, p.79.
7. Linnea Almgren, "May Eve Celebration,' *Thesmophoria*, 3: 8, 9982.
8. Sena, "May Day, Beltane, Roodmas", *Womanspirit*, Vol. 1, No. 3, 1975.
9. Lee Lanning and Vernette Hart, *Ripening* (MN: Word Weavers, 1981).
10. *Wemoon Calendar*, 1989.
11. Linnea Almgren, "Summer Solstice", *Thesmophoria*, 4:1, 1982/9982.
12. Ibid.
13. Story inspired by Moontree.
14. Denise Brown and Dragon, "Wicce 101: The Wheel of the Year," *Goddess Rising*, Brigit 9985.
15. *The Sword of Dyrnwyn Newsletter*, Vol. 2, No. 2, Lammas 9990.
16. Z. Budapest, *The Grandmother of Time*, (NY: Harper & Row, 1989).
17. L. Lanning & V. Hart, *Ripening* (MN: Word Weavers, 1981), p. 20.
18. Cindy Dunigan, *Thesmophoria*, Vol 6, No. 3 9984.
19. Linnea Almgren, *Thesmophoria*, Vol. 4, No. 3, 9982.
20. Judith Laura, *She Lives* , (Freedom, CA: Crossing Pub., 1989) p. 110.
21. This is a true story related to me by my friend Sue Sellars. It contains my embellishments.
22. Patriarchal names: Hallowe'en, Hallomas, Mass of the Dead.
23. Robert Cole, "Your Stars!,' *Santa Cruz Good Times*, Nov. 1979.
24. Excerpt song, Birago Diop ©1980, Barnwell Notes, BMI.

Chapter 5
Lunar Magic

CHAPTER 5 - LUNAR MAGIC

"The importance of moon-time or moon-consciousness is that it consists of such an entirely different attitude than our present solar-centered system. It takes into account the quality of time instead of the quantity. This attitude characterizes our spiritual nature. It is spiritual because the ego waits passively for the favorable time. It puts itself into harmony with the changing moon to bring about unison. Its wisdom is aligned with matriarchal consciousness, the moon-wisdom of waiting, accepting, ripening, and then taking action at the correct time.

"To achieve this inner listening, we need to understand the importance of allowing things to happen in their own time. We need to be patient with ourselves. In woman's primal mysteries, the ritual always centered around a natural cycle: a period of baking, fermenting, ripening, a time of pregnancy before birth, a time of waiting before the transformation became complete.

"What we learn from the lunar cycle is how our outer realities are reflections of inner conditions and how this inner world is constantly shaping the outer world through our sacred Energy, 'chi', or the lifeforce. We need to learn how our Energy flows through our bodies and affects everything around us. Healers have understood this for centuries."[1]

If the year is a song
The moon is the drum beat
marking the rhythm in phases,
changing moods with the signs,
waxing and waning thirteen times, as she circles around.

The Sun is the singer
whose song changes every season
In her relationship with earth
Singing ever new verses of
The twelve tunes of the zodiac
The stars give the melody line
Shaping the notes with their signs
Into patterns the planets play
The planets are the musical tones
We chant, expressing the moments we live.

We are the ones who experience the song of this year
In the notes and melodies we are learning to hear.
We play with the moon, we sing with the sun,
We join in the dance to the music of the spheres.

by Musawa[2]

Daughter of the Full Moon

The Moon cycle spins around to full again, and I find myself in the Moon Circle, living the dream, reaching down into myself for ancient memories of ways to live and be whole.

The circle forms--ten women in all: each seeking her own truths; here together to pay homage to The Divine, The Goddess inside, as well as outside each one. The leadership (Priestess) of the circle has been passed to me, and I ask for the smudging to begin. We smudge each other in turn, to the left, with sage for cleansing and cedar for creating positive vibrations. Each of us gives then receives, holding the sweet smelling herbs over the head of the one on our left, and then up and down her body. The other receives, in meditation and openness, hands outstretched. I beat the drum for the smudging. The Native Peoples say the drum is the heartbeat of the circle, and as I make Her heart beat I remember my years of women's peyote rituals. Tonight my drum becomes our heartbeat.

The five directions, east, south, west, north, center, are addressed, and we ask them to join us on this full moon night. The circle is opened and we are between the worlds--not in this reality--not in the spirit realm--but between, in a place where everyday issues, concerns, and problems are set aside; and gifts from the heart and magical world are our guides.

The chanting begins, and our voices project into the center. I feel the hand of the woman next to me; it is hot with power and life energy. The cone-spiral begins to form; slowly at first, hesitantly; then rising out of the center. I feel the electrical humming and buzzing of that center place where our voices meet, the place where magic is formed. We send the power of the chant to heal our loved ones, ourselves, the earth. Names are called out for those in need of healing and we cast the healing spell.

After this is completed, we ground ourselves, sit, and share the meaning of this moon, called the Maiden Moon. I pass around the writings of the Maiden, and each woman reads out a section. We then share what it means individually, and sing and chant names of Maiden Goddesses: Diana, Artemis, Hina, Lada, Persephone, Kore, Calafia, Mami Watu. I am transformed by the drum, the rattle, and the chants; feeling as if I am "out of myself completely", that I am flying like a bird. I become the heartbeat drumbeat; I can feel it in my pores. I become the rattle shaking, it is now a live thing in my hand: my spirit dances to the shake of the rattling, hissing, twisting snake.

This celebrating, sharing, and music goes on all evening, for hours. I beat the drum the entire time, endlessly. Affirmations are chanted, becoming songs, becoming grapevine dances that move in circles. We hold hands while we move around, and I beat the drum inside the dancing, moving with it. "Happiness, Health and Prosperity," we sing, "For You and Me, Eternally.... for Everyone,

Beneath the Sun.' The words are made up as we go along. The rhyme becomes a chant, becomes a song, becomes a dance. The energy reaches a feverish pitch, and we are transformed by the presence of The Goddess and our own divinity

This is the strongest magic I have experienced in a long time and I am deeply moved. I feel connected in love to everyone here and beyond this room to our Mother, the planet. Our song is for all beings, a song of peace, love, and healing. I wish this experience for everyone, at least once in their lifetime, I am fortunate to have experienced this many, many times. I thank Her who dispenses blessings.

Exhausted, we close the circle. As we do, the Full Moon shows her most beautiful, exquisite face in the glass ceiling of this magic yurt. We chant to Her again, just one last time, and close the circle by grounding and thanking the directions. We repeat three times, 'Merry Meet and Merry Part, and Merry Meet Again'

The feast at the close of the night reflects each woman's caring and love by the food she has prepared for us all. It is, indeed, an evening to remember.

MOON CYCLES

During each lunar month, which begins with the New Moon and ends with the Dark Moon, the moon travels through all the astrology signs, taking 28-29 1/2 days to complete the cycle. Dark Moon is where the waning dark and waxing crescents meet, and is a place of great power, where magical soma essence is generated. This double-helix symbol of the two facing crescents forms the basis for the labrys symbol, also the axe of the amazons, and continues to be reclaimed by contemporary women as a symbol of strength and freedom. The moon's light increases from New Moon to Full, peaks, then decreases from Full to Dark Moon. The cycle then repeats itself.

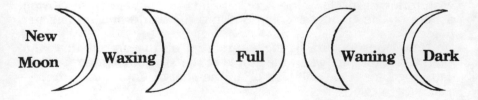

The moon has special power for women, her cycles correspond to our bloods. She represents emotions, fertility, gardens, animals, sexuality, psychic powers and insights. Her light softens differences, and makes visible what is usually invisible, making it possible for us to see ourselves more clearly.

In our culture knowledge of the moon is frequently ignored and suppressed. The lunar calendar was outlawed in 45 B.C.E. by Julius Caesar, and the concept of cyclic process was declared heretical in the 5th century C.E. by the Council of Constantinople. The solar calendar now used ignores the lunar cycle. Rekindling the knowledge of Her cycle will enable us to celebrate life in a more wholistic way. Celebrating the cycles of the moon can be a meaningful way for women to recapture/remember our cyclical skills. We share a common bond with the moon, since our own menstrual cycles correspond to her rhythms.

New Moon/Waxing Crescent

At New Moon the sun and moon rise and set together--we say they are in "conjunction" (within 5 degrees). In this phase we cannot see the waxing crescent at exactly New Moon, but She appears a few days later in the evening sky. Now both the sun and the moon are on the same side of the earth and both in the same astrological sign, pulling us strongly in one direction. This is when we experience a burst of fresh energy and new beginnings, especially when it's in our astrological moon sign.

It is also a time of mystery when the veil between the worlds is thinner, and psychic powers more acute. Like the Full Moon, the New Moon is a time of accentuated highs and lows, although this Moon is more inward and personal than the extroverted Full Moon. Because it is the beginning of a new cycle of growth, it is a good time to "clean up your act", begin new projects, and plant seeds of whatever you would like to come to fruition during this mooncycle. Wishes made when first you see the New Moon will come true. Greet her outside and make a wish, for this is a time to ask for blessings. One old custom is to place a silver coin on a windowsill during New Moon. Show the money to the Moon and ask her to make it grow along with her growth. You can also use other objects symbolizing different aspects of your life that you wish to increase. New Moon corresponds to the Maiden or Nymph aspect of The Goddess, going out into the world and finding her place.

New Moon occurs in the *same* sign as the astrological sun sign. For example, when the sun is in the sign of Capricorn (Dec.-Jan.) the New Moon will also be in the sign of Capricorn.

Waxing Moon

The Waxing Moon, time of enchantment, occurs 2-3 days after the New Moon. This is when the left-facing waxing crescent shows her face in the west. For a two-week cycle of time her light increases (she grows fatter) and energy rises. Everything is active, vital, outgoing and expressive, bringing to fruition the seeds planted at New Moon: a gathering of earth's bounty for health and healing. Each day she **rises an hour earlier** and **sets an hour later.** Halfway through this phase of the cycle the sun and moon are square each other (making a 90 degree angle), bringing challenge and growth through struggle. This moon is visible from noon to midnight. Waxing moon corresponds to Artemis, Goddess of enchantment.

 ### Full Moon

She rises at sunset as the Moon and Sun are on opposite sides of the earth, and in *opposite* astrological signs. For example, Full Moon in Pisces would occur during the sun sign of Virgo (her opposite sign on the zodiac). If the sun sign is in Aries, then the Full Moon will occur in the sign of Libra.

Full Moon is a time in the moon phase of intensity and clarity, strong energies pulling in opposite directions, a time of high creativity, excitement, tension, and tremendous potential, especially if it occurs during your birth sign. The seed of the New Moon is now realized, actualized, and established, and ovulation is stimulated. It is a time to connect psychically with someone you love who is far away, or be your most creative self. Electricity in the air is greatest just before and on the Full Moon; and when she peaks in her fullness, there is actually a sense of relief. Full moon represents maturity, nurturing, and richness; the Mother aspect of the Triple Goddess, Selene and Yemaya, are Goddesses of the Full Moon.

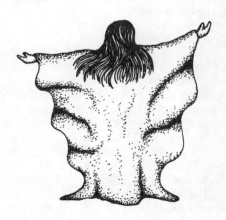

Waning Crescent

During the Waning half-moon crescent, which is right-facing, the Sun and Moon are again square each other at 90-degree angles. Beginning at the Full Moon the moon rises an hour later every night: by half-waning she sets at noon and is visible every morning. The waning crescent symbolizes contraction, inwardness, receptivity, cutting back, and ending the energy begun at the New Moon. It is also a good time for completing, tidying up, or eliminating anything that is no longer necessary. Now we can mentally clean house. It is also a time to share the accomplishments of the preceding Waxing Moon, reap what you sow, weed and prune what you don't need, and clear the way for new energy. This is Goddess as The Crone and The Cutter, She who ends energy with one flash of her scissors or knife. The Goddess Hecate guides us into her cave to rebirth again.

Dark Moon/Balsamic Moon

Dark Moon follows the Waning Crescent phase when the moon disappears, withdrawing and resting. During this time, we often deal with our inner selves and our fears, and take care of all unfinished affairs left from the last moon cycle. This time can be challenging, a time of dreaming, power and quiet. Emphasize resting, watching, listening. It is a time when the soma (life energy) on the planet is released in a power surge.

The lunar-solar New Year starts on the New Moon closest to Winter Solstice, the darkest time for both lunar and solar cycles. It begins a new cycle of growth. The phases of the year correspond to the Moon's phases. New Moon corresponds to Winter Solstice (time of seeding), First Quarter Moon corresponds with Spring Equinox (action), Full Moon corresponds with Summer Solstice (fulfillment), and Last Quarter Moon corresponds with Fall Equinox (re-orientation).

Lunar System

The astrological sun system, which contains twelve zodiacal signs in one year, does not correlate with the lunar system, which contains thirteen cycles of the moon (13 Full Moons, 13 New, 13 Dark). Due to this discrepancy of one unit of measurement, a 'blue moon' occurs once a year, which means that one month contains **two** Full Moons, sometimes in the same astrological sign. For example, in December 1990, there were two full moons; one in the sign of Gemini and one in the sign of Cancer. In 1989, there were two full Moons in the sign of Capricorn; one in June and one in July. A full cycle of moon phases (from New to Full Moon), is called a lunation, or synodic month (approximately 29 days). One cycle of the moon through the signs (approximately 28 days) is called a sidereal month. In one year, there are 13.369 sidereal months. Note: We, as wimmin, bleed in accordance with the sidereal months, or bleed with the phases of the moon and the tides.

The following table shows the different names and energies of each moon cycle. New Moon after Winter Solstice begins the Wheel of the Year.

Celtic Names	Moon	Commonly-Used Names
1 Beth Birch **(First Moon after Winter Solstice)**	Tree of Inception	Cold Moon, Shaman Moon, Rest & Cleansing, Long Nights Moon
2 Luis-Quickbeam	Tree of Life	Earth Renewal Moon, Winter Moon, Quickening Moon
3 Nion Ash	Power of the Sea	Waiting Moon, Wild Moon, Wind Moon
4 Fearn-Alder	Fire Moon	Pele's Moon, Power Moon Storm Moon
5 Saille Willow	Persephone Moon	Maiden Moon, Seed Moon, Budding Trees Moon
6 Uath-Hawthorne	Purification	Reading Moon, Hare Moon
7 Duir Oak	Moon of Great Growing	Blessings/Growing Moon, Mead Moon, Strong Suns Moon,
8 Tinne Holly (Sacred Tree)	Summer Moon Barley Moon	Electric Moon, Bright Moon,
9 Coll Hazel	Concentrated Wisdom	Harvest Moon
10 Muin Vine	Fall Equinox	Mother Moon, Blood Moon
11 Gort Ivy	Ancestors	Resurrection or Joining Moon, Mourning Moon
12 Ngetal Reed	Established Power	Shaman Moon, Working Moon Snow Moon, Long Nights Moon
13 Ruis-Elder	Transformation Death	Crone Moon, Lilith Moon

Gifts (Qualities) of Full Moons

1. Beth Birch: Stillness and knowing, new goals, prosperity, focus, renewal **Goddesses:** Baba Yaga, Chang-O.
    Animal: Spider
2. Luis-Quickbeam: Quickenings, rebirth, purification, initiation. **Goddesses:** Brigit, Kuan Yin, Sarasvati.
    Animal: Dolphin.
3. Nion Ash: Tree of universal magic, rebirth, power of the sea, thunder, On Waiting Moon we are not passive, but gather our powers. **Goddesses:** Februa, Sedna and Anna Perena. **Animal:** Wolf.
4. Fearn-Alder: Tree of resurrection. Spring Equinox, firepower grows, prospers, explores. **Goddesses:** Demeter and Persephone. **Animal:** Ram
5. Saille-Willow: Love and death, Beltane. **Goddesses:** Hecate, Circe, Hera, Persephone, Freya and Hathor. **Animal:** Cow
6. Uath-Hawthorn (Whitehorn): Beginning of summer. **Goddess:** Sacred to Cardea, Goddess of the Hinge, who has the power to open what is shut and shut what is open. She is the beneficiary of craftswimmin and can look backward and forward in time. She is keeper of the four Cardinal Winds.
    Animal: Dove
7. Duir-Oak - Endurance, triumph, turning of the year, midsummer. **Goddesses:** Litha and Selene. **Animal:** Hare
8. Tinne Holly: Time of Artemis, Lammas. **Goddesses:** Habondia, Goddess of Plenty, Corn Mothers, Kore, Ceres, and Cybele. **Animal:** Salmon
9. Coll-Hazel: Poets' tree. Concentrated wisdom, healing. **Goddesses:** Ix Chel and Demeter. **Animal:** Pig
10. Muin-Vine: Joy, exhilaration, wrath, poetry, imagination, richness and crispness, Fall Equinox, Aries Full Moon, (Blood Moon).
    Goddess: Demeter, Goddess of Harvest Moon. **Animal:** Cat
11. Gort-Ivy: Samhain, Goddess as destroyer of life, wisdom, protection, ancestral communication with psychic world, Witches' New Year. **Goddesses:** Hecate and Selket.
    Animal: Snake.
12. Ngetal Reed: Established power, music. **Goddess:** Diana.
    Animal: Owl
13. Ruis-Elder - Friend of family, tree of music, rebirth of Sun, smell of death, tender care to restore mind, body and spirit.
    Goddesses: Baba Yaga and Titania **Animal:** Butterfly.

To understand the energy of the New or Full Moon in each sign, first consult the element that is foremost. This gives the mood of the moon. Full or New Moons in fire signs (Aries, Leo, Sagittarius) give the energy of fire: which is spirit, love, struggle, growth. In earth signs, (Taurus, Virgo, Capricorn), one receives the energy of body, matter, service, form, realism. In air sign Moons (Gemini, Libra, Aquarius), we find gifts of the mind, consciousness, compassion, dispassion. In water sign moons (Pisces, Cancer, Scorpio), the energy flows to us as soul, emotion, sensation, and psyche. "Take the element, the phase of the Moon and the quality, and you'll have a 'feel' for the Moon's energy and essence of the sign. Consult the signs for the essence and put that together with what you already know (phase and element). You can also check your astrological chart to see what house the moon is transiting, and with all this information you will know a lot about the way you will feel."[3] There are certain full moons when we give thanks and ask for our wishes; and these are in the fixed signs of Leo, Scorpio, Aquarius and Taurus.

Monthly Astrological Transits of the Moon

The moon's astrological sign changes every 2 to 2 1/2 days, as she is the fastest moving of all planets in the zodiac. Her lunar transits indicate daily and hourly moods which can change as quickly as the moon's sign. What follows is a description of the general mood and energy apparent during each moon sign.

Days of the month when the transiting moon is in your personal moon sign is a good time to work on your compulsions and unexplainable drives. It is also one of your personal power days. If the transiting moon is conjunct (the same sign and degrees) as your natal sun or moon sign), it will be a time of strength and authority. Eclipses often bring on crises, particularly if they occur during your astrological sign.

You may want to begin creating rituals for times (called returns) when the astrological sign is in the same sign as your sun, moon, and other personal planets. These rituals can give you the opportunity to ground yourself and become attuned to these energies.

Moon in Pisces - Mutable Water Sign - "I believe"

During Moon in Pisces emotional life is more introverted, intuition is at its height and psychic energy is powerful. You are now able to get in touch with your deepest self, but it can also be a time of vagueness, unclarity, and uncertainty. Pisces is about endings as a result of internal processing. With this moon transit I notice a moodiness in others around me, yet it's also an opportunity to fully appreciate art and beauty.

Many wimmin have a good cry with Moon in Pisces, washing away troubles. Or you can be the compassionate friend for a sister who needs to share her troubles. We cry during Moon in Pisces because it's the most watery of all signs. Pisces Moon brings a retreat into the self to do the internal processing and contemplation necessary at least once during the cycle. The outer world 'busyness' becomes fuzzy and vague. Issues are clouded and cold, hard facts slide through your fingers like the slippery fish. Things are not what they seem, so don't be confused by this transit.

Full Moon in Pisces (Virgo Sun) - This is a powerful psychic/spiritual moon and a great opportunity for oracles and divinations: reading tarot, interpreting astrology charts or throwing the I Ching. Psychic and spiritual forces are so strong that a Full Moon ritual is sensitive and magical. However, Pisces is an inner energy, so a solitary ritual would be appropriate, or a small, closely-knit group of good friends, rather than a large gathering.

There is an awareness and appreciation of beauty and art, as well as strong, heightened creativity. Intuition is at its peak in this sign and realization of life's lessons or truths sometimes are unveiled. It's easy to swim around and lose yourself in emotions now, or to escape in books, or other entertainment of a fantastic nature. As the moon floats towards Aries, the mood lifts and becomes more cheerful and outward.

Moon in Aries - Cardinal Fire Sign- "I am"

Moon in Aries is a time of new beginnings, intense activity, pioneering in any field, reaching out with emotional surges, impulsiveness. This moon is the great tester of limits. When the moon is in Aries you may want to depend on yourself, as there is also a certain amount of ego involvement. You might feel impatient now or want to initiate new things.

Aries Moon is based on impulsiveness and acting on feelings of the moment, rather than the result of reason. Sometimes snap decisions are made–later to be regretted. The force of Aries is felt in emotional surges, whereby we are highly assertive and enthusiastic. Aries is known for headstrong behavior, and a tendency towards temperamental blowups. (Now we are susceptible to head injuries.) Selfishness could be an issue, so be extra sensitive to others. This transit is a good time to do skillful work with tools or sharp, cutting instruments.

Full Moon In Aries, called Blood Moon (Libra Sun) - This is a time to reach beyond your usual consciousness and to spend time with both old and new friends. There is a tendency towards losing one's temper, which should be watched carefully, especially as the moon nears Taurus. Since Aries is the sign of the knife, be especially careful with cutting instruments, such as knives, on the Aries blood moon, as cutting tools can draw blood. A Full Moon ritual might concentrate on dealing with outward fire energy in your life. A bonfire is spectacular.

Moon in Taurus - Fixed Earth Sign - "I have"

This lunar transit concerns money, work, property, the body, home and family, sensuality, building cautiously and slowly, being conscientious, growth, sensitivity, planting, and emotional patterns based on security. The energy flow is even and a time for us to experience the sensual.

The forceful forward movement of Aries becomes solid, calm, and patient during Taurus. There is a desire to protect material goods and a strong need for financial security. It is a poor time for change or getting a loan, as people are very cautious and reserved about money, especially during the first part of the transit.

The middle of Taurus is more calm. It is a good time to continue or to finish projects, or to stay at home with family. Taurus gives attention to order and detail. Emotionally, there is stubbornness, but great sensitivity to others. This sensual sign is a good time to appreciate the wonders of the beautiful earth. During a moon in Taurus transit you might want to work in the garden.

Full Moon in Taurus (Scorpio Sun) - A sensuous, grounded full moon ritual should be outside, if possible, and close to the earth, as it is a time of great sensitivity. Bring flowers to the circle.

Moon in Gemini - Mutable Air Sign - "I adapt"

This is a time of communication and other means of expression, freedom, adaptability, short journeys, reading or writing, desire for variety and having more than one thing going at once. You feel talkative and might want to work with your hands during the moon's transit in Gemini.

All communication (talking, writing or reading, and intellectual matters are easier during Gemini Moon. Women are more adaptable and changeable, so take all statements and promises with a grain of salt, especially if the person has proven fickle in the past. It's a hard time to make any decisions, but a good time to use your wit and cleverness in conversation. There is a strong desire for variety and freedom, in emotional matters and in your environment. Issues of the practical world are set aside.

If you're a cautious driver you'll be able to spot the Moon in Gemini by the excessive speed and risk-taking on the road and there are definitely more travellers (short journeys).

Towards the end of the transit, when the moon approaches the sign of Cancer, interactions and communications become more emotional.

Full Moon in Gemini (Sagittarius Sun) - Plan a Gemini full moon ritual that includes talking, singing, and movement.

Moon in Cancer - Cardinal Water Sign - "I feel"

This transit concerns desires about a home, emotional security, entertaining friends, cooking, security issues, nostalgia, and the desire to nurture. Prepare a feast in your home, ask your friends over, or do psychic work together. Women are emotionally and psychically sensitive at this time, and due to these strong emotions it is a "crybaby" moon.

Moon in Cancer brings heightened sensitivity, the desire to nurture, and the need to create a home. Because of the home-orientation, coming from a deep-seated need for security, there is a greater interest in food and its preparation. This can easily lead to self-indulgence, so health-conscious women should be aware of the tendency to food binge. Cancer is the home of the moon, sensitive planet of emotions, so feelings are easily hurt, especially by personal criticism. Handle with care.

For those hoping for children, she is the most fertile sign, and the best time to create new life or growth of any kind. This is not a transit when it's easy to be alone, as needs for security in love and friendship are high. Nostalgia reigns supreme. As the moon moves toward Leo, it is a time of great personal warmth and friendship. Be careful to avoid conflict, as a grudge formed now will take a long time to heal. If you want your hair to grow quickly, have it cut in a Cancer Moon.

Full Moon in Cancer (Capricorn Sun) - This is a wonderful time for an elaborate full moon ritual due to Cancer's sensitivity and psychic attunement.

Moon in Leo - Fixed Fire Sign - "I will"

Dramatic happenings, especially concerning emotions, being the center of attention, exuberance, vitality, and working with patriarchal issues are all hallmarks of the Leo Moon. It's the best time to set appointments within the patriarchal system as this is when we can successfully deal with these issues and people who are in positions of authority and power. It's worth it to reset that appointment, if you can. (Author's note: I have followed this advice, given to me by my first astrology teacher, for 20 years now and never once did it let me down.) Now you can take the direct approach and assert yourself.

It's high drama with the moon in Leo as she steps out onto the stage to entertain us once again. You will probably want to act out the 'drama queen' part of yourself, or just be romantic. This is a time of vital energy, affection, and romance, and a Leo extravaganza. 'Everybody is A Star'. Everyone is recognized for her particular Goddess within. Enjoy the warmth of kindness and generosity, excitement and exuberance, parties and celebrations. You will want to spend money during Moon in Leo.

It's hard to recognize limits in Leo Moon: it's also time for power issues to erupt. Who will be the center of attention? Ambition and independent leadership are important issues. Leo has great pride, which is evident now. As the moon moves to Virgo, the ambitious energy of Leo becomes unassuming.

Leo Full Moon (Aquarius Sun) - On the Leo Full Moon we take a break from growing and hard work to let loose and play. We also get rid of things that are holding us back. A ritual for the full moon in Leo will be a large, lovely drama, emphasizing feelings of warmth and affection. As for power Issues, just make sure beforehand who will be the Priestess and that everyone knows their job.

Moon in Virgo - Mutable Earth Sign - 'I analyze'

During this transit, important issues are practicality, organization, cleaning up your diet or your house, healing your body or offering healing to others and attending to loose ends. After the Leo party, it's time to clean up our act and turn our attentions to the matter of our health and hygiene. Practical Virgo cleans the house, sets things in order, washes the dog, and harvests the vegetables. She purifies and organizes our diet, setting us on the healthy road for the month. It is a time of taking responsibility and cleaning up the messes we've been leaving. Virgo brings painstaking attention to detail; housecleaning is a good way to work through a Virgo transit.

During Virgo Moon, women are mentally active but there is a tendency to excessive criticism both of oneself and others. Emotionally, it's a inward time, when we can reflect on personal relationships.

Virgo Full Moon (Pisces Sun) - Virgo wants to be of emotional service: now is the time to offer this to others. Because there is more inward energy in the universe now, Virgo Full Moon is not the best time for a ritual, unless it's a healing circle which would work just fine! Keep it small.

Moon in Libra - Cardinal Air Sign - 'I balance'

This transit concerns cooperation, harmony, focus on relationships, fine artistic pursuits. When the Moon is in Libra you might enjoy attending an art gallery opening, the opera, or taking your partner to dinner. All partnership activity will be heightened during this moon transit.

But women who are not in a relationship may crave a partnership, or feel alone and lonely. Be aware of superficial bonding just to ease the pain of aloneness. Yet Moon in Libra is a nice time to throw a party. Everyone will be extremely social and try to please and flatter others.

Libra Full Moon (Aries Sun) - During this ritual time, it is important to find balance within the structure. Celebrate, have a party ritual, but also leave time for healing work.

Moon in Scorpio - Fixed Water Sign - "I desire"

The moon's transit through Scorpio is a time of death and rebirth (not necessarily physical death), intensity, extremes, and heightened sensitivity. It is good for focusing, being sexual, and doing psychic work because of the deep emotions and desires Scorpio brings.

Patriarchal astrology paints a grim picture indeed of the Scorpio transit. Since sensitivity is heightened, I find this to be a wonderful time when I can feel the Goddess most intensely, especially the Dark or Crone Goddesses. During Scorpio Moon opinions and feelings are intense and penetrating. Strong desires, especially sexual yearnings, run deep with emotions at their peak.

Emotional resentments from the past can surface and block your heightened creative energy, so fight urges to be suspicious, secretive and moody. This is a time of regeneration and cleaning out of emotional debris from the previous month. There is great energy to complete things and focus on certain areas that you have found yourself too scattered to deal with in the previous cycle. Take the time now for sexual exploration and relaxation.

Full Moon in Scorpio (Taurus Sun) - Scorpio Full Moon rituals are high energy and psychic. The veil is thin between the worlds during Scorpio, and the Goddess joins the circle easily.

Moon in Sagittarius - Mutable Fire Sign - "I seek"

The restless, enthusiastic Sagittarius loves adventure, change and motion. The moon in this sign is a time for philosophy, metaphysics, travelling, studying, and freedom from responsibility.

Sagittarius brings the need to feel free of restrictions, and to be spontaneous. Her restless and independent nature wishes to explore, and warm and friendly vibes make it a good time for seeing new places, encountering different people and relating to a changing environment.

There is a proclivity towards open, honest exchanges. Sagittarius also brings an interest in philosophy, education, ethics, women's culture, and seeing things from an idealistic viewpoint. With this moon transit, comes the itch to travel, and this is the best sign for travel because conditions are most fortuitous, especially for any long, international trips.

Full Moon In Sagittarius (Gemini Sun) - Sag is the best moontime to throw a party, and the full moon is an excellent time to hold a ritual. The spiritual and psychic forces are quite evident now and the desire to connect with the Goddess is strong.

Moon in Capricorn - Cardinal Earth Sign - "I permit"

This transit concerns leadership issues, security, responsibilities, the need to be recognized, desire to create environments, time to take care of business, deal with alternative healing for your body and intensification of your powers of concentration.

After Sagittarius' expansiveness, now we feel contraction and a time to pay attention to our needs for security, duties, obligations, drives and ambitions. It's good for setting and achieving goals, 'going for it" materially; as now we feel persistent and ambitious. It is a bad time to ask or obtain anything from patriarchal and established authorities (do it in Leo) as traditional modes prevail.

Capricorn brings a desire to create environments and energy is slowed down. Be careful to avoid insensitivity to others, and stay out of negative and pessimistic mind sets that will only drag you down. Take this moon transit to deal with your material plane, especially if you have neglected it too long. Do non-traditional healing as Capricorn is the sign of the medicine womon.

Full Moon in Capricorn (Cancer Sun) - At this full moon the goats' horns mirror the ebb and flow of the moon. An old symbol of the goat was the unicorn--someone in charge of their own affairs. Rituals may be hard to get off the ground because of all the grounded earth energy, but they can be a lot of fun once they get going.

Moon in Aquarius - Fixed Air Sign - "I experience"

This is a transit of dealing with facts, organizing, political issues, desire to save the world through social action, connecting with others in social situations, scientific pursuits, detachment, and the need to come and go without restriction.

Aquarius Moon's monthly transit is a dramatic mood change. Where Capricorn values tradition and caution, Aquarius indicates anything new, innovative, different or unconventional. Extremes of behavior occur during this moon, especially extremes of optimism and pessimism. Women feel the need to be friendly and social but don't want to be too personal or go too deep. Aquarius Moon can be detached or rational rather than emotional, and will change only if it's logical to do so. Aquarius is definitely her sister's keeper. She believes "What happens to one woman happens to us all." Freedom is very important now, and you need to live with as few restrictions as possible. Groups play a big part in this moon as Aquarius favors any kind of group interaction, such as a ritual.

Full Moon in Aquarius (Leo Sun) - Be prepared for an electric full moon on a warm, clear August night--brightest moon of the year. Anything can happen; expect the unpredictable.

Interpretation of Natal Moon in the Elements

WATER MOONS

Wimmin with Pisces, Cancer and Scorpio moons are emotional and intuitive, with strong psychic ability. They love the water, especially the ocean, and have a need to live close to it. Water moons love swimming, sailing, and water play.

Pisces Moon wimmin are psychic and impressionable.

Since Cancer rules the Moon, it is exalted here. Cancer Moon wimmin are loving, giving, emotional and affectionate.

Scorpio Moon wimmin are intense, psychic and powerful. Many priestesses and shamans have this moon sign.

AIR MOONS

Gemini, Libra, and Aquarius moons are intellectual wimmin who love to communicate. They are skillful speakers, writers, and poets.

Gemini Moons are excitable and enthusiastic.

Libra Moons crave partnership, and appreciate the finer things in life.

Aquarius Moons are humanistic, altruistic, and cross-cultural, having connections with many different people.

EARTH MOONS

Taurus, Virgo, and Capricorn Moon wimmin are practical and sensuous. They relish the senses of touching, tasting, seeing, smelling and hearing. The earth moons weigh and classify. Many of them are artists, potters, sculptors, and clay workers.

Taurus Moons create beauty to surround them.

Virgo Moons are medicine wimmin, nurses, teachers: anything that makes people more comfortable or equips them for a better life.

Capricorn Moons are business oriented but warm emotionally. They often suffer from fear of rejection.

FIRE MOONS

Sagittarius, Aries and Leo are energetic and active. Generally they are good at starting, bad at finishing, although Leo (fixed fire) finishes. They hate boredom and inactivity.

Sagittarius Moons are creative, love ideas and travel.

Aries Moons often are pioneers, begin relationships easily, but can be selfish.

Leo Moons are babies, but love to love you. They have big hearts and are wonderful drama queens.

PLANTING BY ASTROLOGICAL MOONS

There is a special sympathy and harmony between the Moon, plants and water. Each moon sign lasts approximately 2 1/2 days and it takes approximately 28 days for the moon to complete one cycle. Do not plant anything on the three days before New Moon.

Planting by the moon is done in accordance with the phases of the moon and also by the astrological signs. Above-ground plants are best started during the waxing moon and root crops with the waning moon.

Waxing Moon is a time of new beginnings and growing light. This is the best phase for all plants, but especially above-ground plants where leaves, flowers, stems and fruits are the part of the plant you wish to emphasize.

Waning Moon is when the light decreases. It is a time of contraction, when growth reduces and root crops thrive because they do not have to give as much energy to the other parts.

Because sowing and planting opens the earth to the Moon's rays, there are different seeds we should plant when the Moon is in different elements, according to which part of the plant we want to nourish the most.

Leafy green plants grow best when they are planted in one of the **water sign moons** of Pisces, Cancer, and Scorpio. Some of these plants are spinach, lettuce, leeks, cabbages, chard, kale, and leafy herbs.

The **earth sign moons** of Capricorn and Taurus are the next-best time to plant stem and leaf plants. In Virgo, Taurus, and Capricorn, plant any vegetable that needs a big root to grow, such as onions, garlic, carrots, beets, potatoes, turnips, and radishes.

Fire and air sign moons are not good for planting, except for the air sign of Libra, which is good for planting flowers. The Gemini Moon transit can be a time for weeding, pruning, and getting rid of garden pests.

MOON GARDENS
Adapted from the writings of Joan Anderson[4]

To sprout and grow, a seed needs water, good temperature, and oxygen. In the spring, old wise wimmin tell us to plant when the moon is waxing in the first quarter and in the sign of Cancer, if possible, or another water sign. From their advice we can glean a set of relationships that will guide planting by the moon: the relationship of earth and plant to the sun and the season, of earth and plant to the moon (first quarter waxing), and the relationship of earth and plant to astrology.

The phases of the moon echo the four seasons. During the "Spring" quarter, the moon waxes from new to half-full. During the "Summer" quarter, the moon waxes from half-full to full. In "Autumn" quarter, the moon wanes from full to half-full. During "Winter" quarter the moon wanes from half-full back to dark.

As a general rule of thumb, when we desire plants with leaves or above ground parts, we sow their seeds during waxing moon. When the moon is waning, we sow seeds for plants with tubers and underground parts.

Coordination of the moon's phases, the part of the plant desired, the moon's zodiacal sign, and the elemental nature of the zodiacal sign (see previous section on Astrological Moon planting) can enhance the ability of plants to grow to perfection, withstanding drought, pestilence and onslaughts of weather.

THE ECSTASY OF LUNA[5]
By Mara Meshak

Since I've lived most of my life in cities, I rarely saw the moon except for the accidental glimpses of her through the chinks in the buildings. I became preoccupied by my own "inner moon" cycle, realizing that my individual rhythms were connected with a universal experience. Now that I live in a place where I can see the beautiful body of the changing moon, I can recognize her nature in myself and in other women, and I rejoice in her graceful reminder of the mysteries of life and rebirth, too easily forgotten in this culture. My womanvision of Luna extends through history and unites me with other women who praised her more boldly and openly, and called her by name. My intuitions about her are by no means a "rule" or a "system" for all women, but present my personal groupings to attune myself with her nature. This is my vision:

Within the cave of Night, Isis, the one-eyed cat mingles with the shadows. The slit of her eye widens to the darkness, it becomes a dull fathomless pearl as she slinks deeper into the recesses, and when she crouches in the Underworld her eye is a sunken and haggard red.

Veiled in the day, she is called Mystery, or 'seen-with-the-eyes-shut'. The Moon initiates women into the mysteries of Isis who is the rhythm and form of womanlife. The Dark Crescent shows her aspect as psychic Virgin, one-in-herself, the Lady of the Wild Things who delights in untamed nature. Her crescent is the bow of Artemis, the divine Huntress who sweeps across the forests and waters, stirring to life those things that are in seed. Her Amazon daughters dwell on the frontiers, and on the islands of the edge of civilization, and protect her from domesticity. She who tramples fences and boundaries and who loves beginnings and storms is called Omphale, Diana, Atlanta, Lilith. We womyn are introduced to our power with our first menstrual blood flow when we join with the tides, the seasons, and the dance.

The Waxing Moon is the Lover, she who swells and draws things to grow through love. She is The Corn Mother to the Pawnee and is known as Demeter when she recalls her daughter from the wintry underworld. Her women are planters, potters, and keepers of the hearth flame. She gives her daughters the mothersecrets of the kettle and of the cauldron, vessels of transformation. When she suckles, her babes call her Hathor the cow-mother or Cybele, mother of Itomo.

Ritual for Drawing Down the Moon

Drawing Down The Moon can take place during a moon circle with a group, or be a private ritual with yourself. I prefer to be outside, under the Full Moon. But if that is not possible, it can also take place inside, sitting, standing or facing a window, with the moon's rays shining in on you.

Start by chanting 'Ma', 'Yemaya', or 'Luna' for five or ten minutes, to raise energy for the drawing-down. Place your hands with palms facing the moon, index fingers and thumbs touching, forming the sacred triangle, or sign of the yoni. Spread your fingers as wide as possible, so they are receptors for moon energy. After you chant to raise power, focus all your energy and vision on Mother Moon and draw her energy down into your body. Move your hands, if desired, back and forth, froman arms-outstretched position to your heart and back again. After a few minutes of holding your hands up to the moon, you can feel them tingle. This is magical energy. I usually take 15-20 minutes

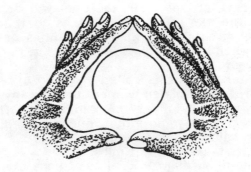

to draw her into me, but you may take more or less time, there are no rules. Here are some songs and chants to the moon:

"Yemaya, O Lo Do, Agua, Lo Do Mi O"
(repeat over and over)

"Moon, Moon, Moon on my mind, think I'll fly"
(repeat over and over)

The moon goes through Her glorious cycles of new, full, and dark, just as we women go through our transformations from young woman (Maiden), to middle age (Mother), and finally to old woman (Crone or Hag). Lunar cycles and phases once marked the passage of time. Now solar calendars invented by patriarchy are exclusively used as our timekeeping instruments, ignoring lunar time and lunar consciousness.

Moon Celebrations
by Baba Copper

The Soma of the Moon is the fruit of each lunar cycle for the healing of all living things. Within five degrees of Dark Moon is the time of maximum Soma. By understanding and celebrating together the waxing and waning of the lunar cycle, wimmin can tune themselves to her rhythms.

During the waning cycle, the Soma generates and grows, accumulating in all water, plants, and animals. The change of the cycle from waning to waxing, at Dark Moon, is a time for celebration of the greatest Soma--a vibration which is stable, focused and powerful. It is the Time of Transformation.

During the waxing cycle, the Soma is externalized through event formation and actions. The change of the cycle from waxing to waning at the Full Moon, is a time for celebrating the ending of a full cycle–a Time for Integration. It is a vibration which is unstable, sensual, emotional and fecund.

These two times of celebration, with their different flavors of energy, can be used by wimmin as group times to pulse with the Moon. There is power to be had from Moon resonance in the company of other wimmin, and there is healing. Finding spots in Nature of high telluric charge where we can celebrate is important. Celebrating inside homes is good. Creating a permanent shrine to the Moon in an energy spot, where wimmin can come at any time to be resourced, is also good. Celebration of the Moon should be joyous—with eating, dancing, caressing, music, holding each other, and dreaming (Dream Circles of Sleep) as part of the high. Every moment of the time should be crowded with shared energy, communication and nurturance—with every womyn participating fully in the magical experience.

To this end, it is necessary that the pace be guided by one or two wimmin, using a bell for interruption and centering, who bear the responsibility for guiding the group energy. This role can circulate through the group.

All Moon Celebrations are a time for:

Meditating together, with silent-witness-of-the-moon being our center. Ritualized touching and laying-on of hands. Chanting together, finding Syllables and Sounds of Power. Earth-Listening and North-Pointing--tuning to the Earth. Communication about our menses, trying to bring them together and with the moon (post menopausal and pre-menstrual wimmin will observe their sexual cycles also and share information with the others.)

The Full Moon, the Celebration of Integration can be:

A time of telling tales to each other, making up myths, boasting, show and tell, poetry, self-expansive pride and shouting, exhibitions of self in any form.

A time to tell each other the new things we are learning about healing, diet, plants and animals, our bodies, and the use of time.

A time of symbolic rebirthing--with the group or as an individual.

A time to Eye-Share--one to one, staring into each other's left eye, looking for the other lives lurking there.

A time to cast Invocations of Power against patriarchal oppression. Naming what oppresses us and using our anger as part of our power.

A time to agree on desired events. How do we detach ourselves from the system? How do we deny them access to our bodies and our spirits? How do we create our own communities and institutions?

The Dark Moon, Celebration of Transformation, can be:

A time of honoring our foremothers and our own mothers; telling what they did, why they were important, and the good things they gave to us.

A time for healing, closeness, touching, comforting, sharing focused energy, massage and laying-on of hands.

A time for sharing pain—talking about death, self-hatred, suicide, survival, separations, ageing, paranoia, dis-ease, wounds and worries. A healing time.

A time for guided Imagery and group energy, visualizations.

A time to value each other--talking about the things we know about each other, speaking out our love, admiration, identity with and empathy for each other.

LUNAR RESONANCE FOR WOMEN
A Meditational Method for the Evolution of Consciousness
By Baba Copper - In Memorial (slightly revised)

This system is a powerful method and I have benefited from it many times. It is my memorial to Baba Copper.

Lunar Resonance is a method for tuning to the energy of the Moon. By focusing attention on the power latent in the lunar cycles, and by accurate resonant timing, women can tap the evolutionary potential of that energy to a far greater degree than with ordinary meditation methods. The 9+9 resonant timing is a rhythm of induced positive feedback similar to pushing a swing forward at precisely the correct moment to enhance acceleration.

Nine days of the Waning Moon (the Inner Life) and nine days of the Waxing Moon (the outer life) have a specific energy potential which was recognized and tapped by women in ancient times. Hints of this forgotten knowledge exist in many patriarchal esoteric traditions, but the lost method of timing has only recently been rediscovered. The lunar energy flow (Soma) is the "Tree of Life" which bears leaves each month for the healing of all living things--but is accessible only through awakened awareness in a state of meditation and receptivity.

When the Sun and the Moon are in conjunction (Dark Moon), the Soma is strongest. The Double Ax is one symbol for this point of maximum lunar power, showing the waning and waxing crescents abutting. The time of minimum Soma in the lunar cycle is at Full Moon, a time of instability.

Soma is the life-restoring, immortalizing energy which can activate in humans the etheric body which survives death. It is present in all living things in varying degrees. Psychedelic plants are called Soma plants. The fruit of the Moon tree or Soma

Drink is brewed from them. Soma accumulates in all water, plants, and animals.

The Waning Moon is the power-generating, charging phase of the double helix. It is a time of growth of inner insight and intuition. The Waxing Moon is the power-externalizing, form-manifesting phase of the double helix. The Soma gathered in the Waxing Moon can be focused in positive attitudes and beliefs resulting in health of the physical body and harmony in the event-formations of the outer life.

Oobies, or "out of body" experiences, are the temporary separation of the etheric body from the physical body, while the mind remains alertly conscious throughout. Oobies can occur at any phase of the lunar cycle.

How to Identify the 9+9 Moondays of Vibrant Meaning

To find the time of the Inner Power-generating Waning Moondays, and the Outer Power-expressing Waxing Moondays, use the following method:

Obtain the date of the current Full Moon from an almanac, newspaper, or observatory. (A Moonday begins and ends at dawn. Full Moons between midnight and dawn are counted as occurring one day earlier--with dawn occurring two hours before sunset.) The first day **after** the day of the Full Moon is **Moonday #1**.

For the complete series, use the following table.

Moonday #	Day After Full Moon								
	1	2	3	4	5	6	7	8	9
Waning	1st	2nd	3rd	5th	7th	8th	9th	11th	13th
Waxing	16th	17th	18th	20th	22nd	23rd	24th	26th	28th
	Day After Full Moon								

You now have **waning** Moonday #1 as the 1st day after the Full Moon. Waning Moonday #4 is the 5th day after the Full Moon, **waxing** Moonday #2 is the 17th day after Full Moon, **waxing** Moonday #5 is the 22nd day after Full Moon., etc. You will now have a set of 9 Moondays for each Waning Cycle and 9 Moondays for each Waxing Cycle. There are some days, as you can see, that you will not meditate at all. The first 3 days of the Waxing Cycle you do, then you skip a day, and do again. You then skip a day. Moondays #1, 2, 3, 5, 6 and 7 are done three in a row. There is a two-day break between Waning Moonday #9 (day 13) and Waxing Moonday #1 (day 16).

If you should have to omit any sessions, be sure to include at least Moondays #1, 4, 5, 8, and 9 of each two week period. Always start (or resume) the day after the Full Moon.

How to use Lunar Resonance Meditation

This is a method of helping meditation to work by accurate, resonant timing. Each Moonday of the 9+9 cycle has an essence. By quieting or slowing the mind and letting the abiding feelings which the essence of the Moonday evoke in you and fill you, you become open to the Soma available at that time. By remembering the intent or meaning of the essence of the Moonday occasionally throughout the day, the meditation is reinforced.

Meditate at a regular, convenient time—upon rising, at sunset, or before going to sleep. During the Waning Moon, face West, the place of moonset; during the Waxing Moon, face east, place of the dawn.

Begin on the **Waning** Cycle. On Moonday #1, do meditation #1, on Moonday #6, do meditation #6 (#6 is the 8th day **after** the Full Moon). You will reach the **Waxing** Cycle (Waxing Moonday #1) on the 16th day after Full Moon and will begin with the Waxing meditations. Continue until the next Full Moon, then begin again.

MOONDAY ESSENCES
The Waning Inner Power-generating Fortnight

1) **Rededication** to my own inner growth. A time of purposefulness and high expectation. By becoming aware of my potential to develop and perfect a consciously accessible etheric body, I activate the energy patterns in my brain which will perfect such a vehicle. My potential and the deep aspirations within me to fulfill that nature, are evoked.

2) **Access** between my left brain and my right brain, between my ego and the inner knowing, between the dreaming self and the waking self, between the conscious and the unconscious. A time when the memories and resources of the Other-Way-of-Knowing are more accessible to me.

3) **Power of the Unconscious.** Habits of attitude or feeling which block my development can be released through the latent power of this Moonday to change the force-patterns of emotion and belief in my unconscious self. Deep root-growth will result in unknown benefits.

4) **Soma Absorption Toward Oobies.** This Moonday provides the energy to my etheric body which will eventually enable me to function outside my physical body. Higher life energies reawaken the growth of my inner body. Freedom for the etheric body is easier on this Moonday.

5) **Honest Self-Scrutiny.** I can see myself with clarity and honesty. I can change those aspects of myself which I do not like. On this moonday I will find more aspects of myself which agree with my potential.

6) **Insight.** The power that flows on this Moonday enables me to combine intuition and rationality. The information I gain from empathy, telepathy, and all other extrasensory channels merges with my logical focus without resistance, resulting in creativity.

7) **Vision.** The power to see far beyond myself, to know that which I do not know, to experience an inward certainty that I am becoming who I truly am. The strength of higher vision available to me on this moonday sustains my ability to find all the opportunities latent in my experience.

8) **Climax of the Accumulation Of Soma.** This Moonday is very close to maximum Soma for the freeing of the etheric body. The Moon energy that my aware attention has accumulated throughout the fortnight is released in a climax of inner change which brings me one step nearer to a conscious transcendence of physical death.

9) **Preservation of Soma Change.** The protective energy available this moonday seals the life energies I have gained in the previous eight moondays. The changes are absorbed into the center of my being where they work quietly for inner growth.

MOONDAY ESSENCES
The Waxing Outer Power-expressing Fortnight

1) **Engaging Life.** I begin to spin Ariadne's thread of harmonious life choices from the vital energy of this fortnight of moondays. On this particular moonday, my breath, my speech, my body movements and all other conscious body functions gain in health and effectiveness.

2) **Power Connections.** My conscious and unconscious body functions are able to use the energy of this moonday to link more fully with each other and to harness themselves to the Other-Way-of-Knowing. All artistic creativity in movement, sound, or space flourishes this moonday, as well as yogic disciplines of meditation, breathing, and autonomic control.

3) **Power.** The energy of this moonday provides the power I need to activate conscious event-formation, which will be helpful in my near future. Also, health and help are given to autonomic body functions of the organs, glands and the nervous system.

4) **Energy Peak.** The Soma of this moonday is strong, making it a time for rebirth and change in my body and outer life. I can use this day to shed old patterns, start anew, initiate, and redeem.

5) **Cleansing.** This is a moonday of self-cleansing energy. The shedding of wastes of the body or undesirable situations of my life is desirable and easier at this time. Elimination processes

are activated which result in new body energy and strength, aiding me until this time of the next month. Baths, herb teas and medicines, and cleansing rituals are especially effective on this day.

6) **Clarification.** Love-power permeates all event-formation underway on this moonday and transfuses the body with the very Root of Grace.

7) **Abundance of Power**. My reserves of luck and health-energy are replenished on this moonday. Difficult things can be done more easily.

8) **Blessing.** This is a time of grace, nearing the full moon, which will help my body and the event-formations of my outer life, causing my environment to agree with me.

9) **Preservation of Achievement.** On this moonday the renewed strength of my body and outer life which I have gained from the energy of the previous eight moondays is seed-planted deep within me. I recognize and preserve my achievement.

Notes - Chapter 5

1. Ann Filemyr, *Matriarchal Consciousness: Healing The Bodyspirit Split,* Lady-Unique-Inclination-Of-The-Night, Autumn 1978, pgs. 40-41.
2. *Wemoon Calendar,* 1989, (Consult The Bibliography. to order).
3. Norma Joyce, *Wemoon Calendar,* 1984, p. 18.
4. *Womanspirit Magazine,* Spring Equinox, 1976, Vol. 2, #7.
5. *Llewellyn's 1979 Moon Sign Book,* Bantam Books, Toronto, N.Y.,London, 1979.

BIBLIOGRAPHY

Stephen Arroyo, M.A., *Astrology, Psychology and the Four Elements,* (Vancouver, WA.:CRCS Publications, 1975).

Stephen Arroyo, M.A., *Relationships and Life Cycles,* (Vancouver, WA.: CRCS Publications, 1979).

Catherine Bowman, *Crystal Awareness,* (MN: Llewllyn, 1988).

Page Bryant, *Crystals and Their Use,* (Albuquerque, NM.: Sun Books, 1984).

Z. Budapest, *The Holy Book of Women's Mysteries, Part I and II,* (Los Angeles, CA.: Susan B. Anthony Coven #1, Member of COG, 1980).

Z. Budapest, *The Grandmother of Time,* (N.Y.: Harper and Row, 1989).

Martha Courtot, *Tribe,* (San Francisco. CA.: Pearlchild, 1977).

Janet and Stewart Farrar, *The Witches' Goddess,* (WA.: Phoenix Pub. Inc., 1987).

Liz Greene, *Astrology for Lovers,* (York Beach, Maine: Samuel Weiser, Inc., 1980).

Mary Greer, *Tarot Constellations,* (North Hollywood, Newcastle Publishing, 1987).

Robert Hand, *Planets in Transit,* (Rockport, MA.: Para Research, Inc., 1976).

Margaret E. Hone, D.F. Astrol. S., *The Modern Text Book of Astrology,* (London: L.N. Fowler and Co. Ltd., 1951).

Sonia Johnson, *Wildfire,* (Albuquerque, NM.: Wildfire Books, 1989).

Lee Lanning and Vernette Hart, *Ripening,* (MN.: Word Weavers, 1981); *Dreaming,* (1983); *Awakening,* (1987).

Judith Laura, *She Lives! The Return of Our Great Mother,* (Freedom, CA.: Crossing Press, 1989).

Diane Mariechild, *Mother Wit,* (NY.: The Crossing Press Feminist Series, 1981).

Sherry Mestel, *Earth Rites,* (N.Y.: Earth Rites Press, 1978).

Vicki Noble and Jonathan Tenney, *Motherpeace,* (San Francisco, CA.: Harper and Row, 1983).

Vicki Noble, *The Motherpeace Tarot Playbook,* (Berkeley, CA.: Wingbow, 1986).

Robert Pelletier, *Planets in Aspect,* (Rockport, MA.: Para Research, 1974).

Phoenix and Barbel Messmer, *Venus ist Noch Fern,* (Munchen: Come Out Lesbenverlag, 1979).

Catherine Ponder, *Open Your Mind to Prosperity,* (Marine del Rey, CA.: De Vorss and Co., 1983).

Dorothy Riddle and Robert Dobson, *Our Birth Charts,* (Tucson, AZ.: Minerva Astrology Center, 1974).

Diana Rivers, *Journey to Zelindar,* (Denver, CO.: Lace Pub., 1987).

Anne Kent Rush, *Moon, Moon,* (NY.: Random House, 1976).

Michael G. Smith, *Crystal Spirit,* (MN.: Llewellyn, 1990).

Marcia Starck, _Earth Mother Astrology_, (St. Paul, MN.: Llewellyn, 1989).

Starhawk, _Truth or Dare_, (San Francisco, CA.: Harper & Row, 1987); _The Spiral Dance_, (1979).

Diane Stein, _The Women's Book of Healing_, (MN.: Llewellyn, 1987); _The Women's Spirituality Book_, (1987); _A Women's Book of Ritual_, (Freedom, CA.: Crossing Press, 1990).

Merlin Stone, _Ancient Mirrors of Womanhood_, (Village Station, N.Y.: New Sibylline Books, 1979).

Geraldine Thorsten, _God Herself_, (N.Y.: Doubleday and Co., Inc., 1980).

Richard Blackmore Vaughan, _Astrology in Modern Language_, (N.Y.: G.P. Putnam's Sons, 1972).

Wabun and Sun Bear, _The Medicine Wheel_, (New Jersey, Prentice Hall Inc., 1980).

Barbara Walker, _Women's Rituals_, (San Francisco: Harper and Row, 1990).

Valerie Worth, _The Crone's Book of Wisdom_, (MN.: Llewellyn, 1989).

Zolar, _The Encyclopedia of Ancient and Forbidden Knowledge_, (Los Angeles: Nash Publishing, 1970).

MAGAZINES AND NEWSLETTERS

Philip Burbutis, (compiler), _Quartz Crystals for Healing and Meditation_ (Taylor, AZ.: Universarian Foundation Inc., 1976).

Fireheart, No. 4, (Maynard, MA., 1989).

The '85 Lunar Calendar, (Boston, MA.: Lunar Press, 1985).

Of a Like Mind, Vol. 3, No. 4, (Madison, WI., 9986).

Reclaiming Newsletter, (San Francisco, CA., 1982).

SageWoman, Vol. 3, Issue 9, (Santa Cruz, CA., May 9989).

Ila Suzanne, _There Will Be Signs_, (Portland, OR., 1986); _They Gathered in Groves_, (San Diego, CA., 1986).

The Sword of Dyrnwyn, Vol. 3, No. 3, Lammas and Autumn Equinox, (Marietta, Georgia, 1990).

Tarot Interpreter, Vol. 1, No. 3, (Sugar Creek, Missouri, October 1988).

Tasha, _An Introduction to Quartz Crystals_, (1986).

Thesmophoria, (Oakland, CA., 1982-1990).

Kay Turner, (ed.) _Lady Unique Inclination of The Night_, (Autumn, 1978).

We'moon Calendars, 1984-1990. To obtain, contact: Mother Tongue Ink., 37010 S.E. Snuffin Rd., Estacada, OR. 97023.

Woman of Power, Spring, (Cambridge, MA., 1984).

Womanspirit, (Wolf Creek, OR., 1975-1984).

Women in Constant Creative Action, _On Wings_, (Eugene, OR., 1986-1987).